CW00840465

ROGER FEDERER: 20 GRAND SLAMS

A LOOK BACK AT HIS MAJOR VICTORIES

LUCIANO LAMUCCA

CONTENTS

© Copyright 2019 - All rights reserved.

It is not legal to reproduce, duplicate, or transmit any part of this document in either electronic means or in printed format. Recording of this publication is strictly prohibited and any storage of this document is not allowed unless with written permission from the publisher except for the use of brief quotations in a book review.

INTRODUCTION

People love sports, and they love them for a reason. Athletes and their results inspire hope in people. They inspire it because of their struggle, and feats they achieve as a result are amazing. Whether it's football or basketball, each win inspires something in the human soul which can never be extinguished. And, the connection becomes even more significant when you take a look at the individual sports.

Individual sports are all about personal effort. It means the world to people to find somebody they can relate to on a personal level. So, when you think about such great athletes, you have to think about tennis players. And, one of them that stands out is Roger Federer.

Federer was born on 8.9.1981 in Basel, Switzerland. Even though he was proclaimed unfit to serve in the military, he proved formidable in sports. In the early years, he played badminton and basketball, which he would later credit as detrimental for his success in sports. But, this all is just biographical trivia, which doesn't disclose much about him. More or less, he had a normal life before turning pro in 1998. Yet, to truly understand a man's life and career achievements, you should look at the true genesis of his being a professional sportsman. Here, you'll be able to read all about his conquest. But you can find something more.

The greatest problem with biographical works on professional athletes is that it misses the very core of the people behind the brand. Today, athletes aren't just players who devoted years to practice and sport. They are looked at, understood, and seen as almost corporate entities. Thus, you get to love a particular player until he fills his purpose, and is replaced by a new generation of players. Looking at how people came to be who they are, gives you a glimpse into their soul and rewards you with a chance to grow by learning. When you hear their battles, strife, and adversities they faced, you get inspired to grow personally. Even more so, it allows you to love the player when you meet them one on one. When you witness the scale of their adversity and what they went through, you'll get a glimpse of what it takes to be a pro.

Federer is an excellent example of that. Entering the professional world meant everything for him from a very young age. When the shot came in 1998, it wasn't like everything fell into his lap. He struggled. He had to fight a bad temperament, which was a result of his lack of confidence. It led him to break a lot of rackets and earn a bad reputation with the audience. During the next five years, he would win and lose without a sheer perspective on his career. Some believed he was insanely talented. Others thought he wouldn't make it far. Yet, it all changed in 2003, when he won his first Grand Slam at Wimbledon. From that point on, his life changed forever. He would win many tournaments, become a legend of the sport, and achieve a lot as an athlete. Later on, he would participate in philanthropy and charity work, help those in need, and became a brand ambassador for many businesses. But that's what's happening today. Back in the day, in that now-distant 1998 nobody knew that such a prosperous fate awaited young Federer. Even though his talent was imminent, the point is that talent is never enough. It's the work that makes a person reach the stars.

That's what this book is all about. Sure, there's going to be biographical data, but you are going to get a peek into Federer himself. Here you'll get to share the strife, adversity, and overwhelming feeling of victory with the great Roger Federer. This book will inspire you also to pick up a racket. It will at least when you get to meet the ups and downs that made Roger Federer who he is today. Once you read this, you'll see what it took for him to get where he is today.

Having a chance to connect with someone who personally achieved a lot gives you an opportunity also to improve. Let's take a step back from the sportsmen and focus on the audience. The reason sports arenas and stadiums are full for centuries is simple. People love adversity, and even more, people love others who overcome adversity. Human beings are wired in a way that they are easily uplifted when they see others trying their best.

Whether you are a tennis enthusiast, a sports fan, or someone just trying to get further in life, or a person looking to get out of the rut, this book is for you. After you witness the rise of one of the greatest men in contemporary sport, you won't be left dissatisfied. In the end, it all comes down to what you expect as a reader. Whatever it is, at least you'll get an interesting, informative read. Learn everything about Federer's participation in Grand Slams, what was happening with him during his formative years, and how he made it to the top. Finally, get a glimpse into the moments that made him the athlete he is today, and which were the moments that made it so.

The only thing left is to meet the man himself. It all started in 2003 at Wimbledon, where Federer's legend began.

CHAPTER ONE: GRAND SLAM 1

IT ALL STARTED AT WIMBLEDON 2003

In the history of any sport or athlete, there's a moment of breakthrough. Whether it's a boxer, golfer, or a tennis player, there comes the point of their career when nothing remains the same. It's a moment when a previously struggling player enters the mainstream and gets the recognition he rightfully deserves. For Roger Federer, that moment came at Wimbledon in 2003.

At just 21 years of age, Federer won his first Grand Slam. Insanely talented and furiously tempered, he had his streak of losses before the big win. This first big victory was quite different than anything before in his career. Yet, to fully encapsulate the actual rise, the genesis of the great athlete, we have to go way back into his life.

Even as a teenager, Roger had a dream of holding a golden trophy at Wimbledon. Heading from Switzerland, young Federer showed his talents early on. Everything about him pointed out that he was going to be an athlete. Even though he looked slim, he was athletically gifted. Additionally, he had a great balance between his limbs and a proportional leg and arm strength to par. Also, he had promising stamina that proper conditioning would take him to the heights of the sport. During the army recruitment process, he lacked a lot to be a professional soldier. But, for professional tennis, there was a foundation to build upon. Only the building process was left. For the young legend in the making, every day was set about reaching that dream. So, he ground with fervor day in and day out. His first chance came in 1998 and 1999 when he transitioned from junior to professional tennis. It was a matter of months before he entered the top 100 and reached a stunning number 29. However, not all were peaches and cream for the young legend in the making.

His temper, which he had trouble controlling, earned him a bad reputation. In those first pro career matches, he didn't seem to have the mental strength and willpower for longer games. He would easily get flustered and get a notorious reputation for breaking rackets either mid-game or after it. Tennis is a sport for gentlemen, and gentlemen don't support that behavior at the court. To top it all, he wasn't coming to Wimbledon in the highest of graces.

On the contrary, the match-ups from 2001 up to 2003 made him look highly inconsistent. In 2001 he defeated then No.1 Junior with ease. All those things critics would praise him for came to light. The smooth game, the fine arsenal of techniques, the strong serve, all came together in the form of a fantastic victory he won. Yet, it wasn't something he could maintain. During those two years, he would win and lose multiple matches, with his most significant loss in the first round of Wimbledon in 2002. For most observers, it didn't look like he would win the tournament in 2003.

As he would climb and win against other competitors, other problems also plagued Federer. After a string of good match-ups, and Lleyton Hewitt losing to Ivo Karlovic, Federer faced another great player, Feliciano Lopez. You would recall reports of a negative head-to-head between Federer and Feliciano Lopez before the match. During that match, Federer felt a sharp pain in his upper back. His coach looked at him, and would later admit in the interview that it was a turning point for him. And that's the beauty of sports. There, in those moments of complete strife, complete adversity, comes a moment when a man gets to measure himself. His coach would later recall that after that, a sharp pain ran through his back, he could back down. Like many times before, he could get emotional, break down, and destroy his racket. Yet, he didn't. After the break, his eyes looked different. They had a new glow and new strength. He was on a mission to win. Set after a set, he knew, yet something was amiss. Nobody knew that at that moment, a legend was born. The next match would set the tone for it all.

In the next match, he would encounter a star, Andy Roddick, which was the beginning of a great rivalry. Roddick would jokingly say that "Federer beat him to a pulp," but little did he know. Going forth, Roddick would lose a bunch of matches in his later career. The cruelty of the world is finely presented in sports. For some to rise, the others must lose. For one to acquire the grace of victory, the other must lose it. Andy Roddick was an amazing player, yet this would be the beginning of his fall from grace, which would be later fortified with the ascension of the big three, including Federer, Nadal, and Djokovic. The semi-final match was long-awaited. Both players entered the semi-finals with relative ease. The press coverage made this almost a cinematical showdown between two greats, before meeting the great "Scud" in the finals. Whoever won would meet Mark Philippoussis for the golden trophy. The first set was close and went to a tie break. In the tiebreak, Roddick held set point at 6–5, however, he would commit a forehand error into the net and Federer would go on to win the set, and the match 7–6, 6–3, 6–3. Everything was set for the first of many Wimbledon wins.

Then, it finally came: the match that pushed Federer to stardom. And it wasn't an easy one. His opponent Mark Philippoussis had a nickname "the Scud." That name was up to par since he had a serve that felt like a missile. Well, Philippoussis says, ever since that first visit I've wanted to win here, it's so special." It wasn't by chance or luck that he came to the finals. Here, the Scud looked like a promising winner. With his earlier games and upsets, it seemed natural that he would win. And that's why people love sports and its heroes so much. It's at that exact moment Federer put everything on the line. Observing the situation from the Scud's perspective, the win was important. However, he had a great career so far, and a single loss wouldn't phase him as much. For Federer, this was a detrimental moment in his career. If he won, this would be the first Grand Slam he won in his life, and it would be a sign of things to come. Young and with his soul on fire hidden between that common Swiss coldness, he entered the court.

The moment they met, the Scud didn't know that he wasn't facing a hot-tempered, insecure Federer. This was the new Federer, the Federer that had a new fire in his eyes. That's why sports are so amazing. It may be only a single moment, but it comes where all about the player comes together. All those talents, tricks, techniques, came together, and he dismantled the Scud. Of course, the match wasn't without epic drama of its own.

The game didn't start too great for Federer. The Scud, as the name suggests, had some fantastic serves. In the first few sets of games, three out of five serves were unreturnable. However, Federer had plans of his own. He takes the set in the tie break and makes the Scud get all the more serious. The Scud managed to make it even in the next few games, but to no avail. With his height and build, he was known to break in the middle of the game. For Federer, it was a second to capitalize. Whatever Scud threw at him, Federer countered and returned double. Federer won the first set, and things already looked bleak for the Scud. Yet, he insisted on staying in the game. But, it was to no avail.

The second set was complete Federer dominance. Philippoussis literally couldn't do anything. He ultimately lost the set, and couldn't regain composure for the rest of it. So, they ventured into the third set. Here, Philippoussis regained composure briefly. But it was too late. Federer was proclaimed a winner after the third set.

In a sigh of relief, Federer says, "There was pressure on all sides, and it's a huge relief to win. I just hope it won't be my last: "I was always joking when I was a boy that I would win this," Federer said amidst tears as he prepared to receive the trophy.

It wasn't long after that Federer would take the first golden Grand Slam trophy in his hands. After years and years of hard work, it all came to fruition. He finally won a Grand Slam, and he couldn't keep the tears from his eyes. But those were tears of joy, nothing was ever the same, and the legend was born. That day he found out two things about life. How it feels to hold that trophy, and that dreams do come true.

Summary:

- Final: beat Mark Philippoussis 7-6(5) 6-2 7-6(3)
- Games won/lost: 136/81
- Sets lost: 1
- Total time on court: 12 hours 25 minutes
- Top 10 opponents defeated: Andy Roddick (world No 6)
- Coach: Peter Lundgren
- Federer said: "Just to be on the board with Bjorn Borg and these people, it's incredible to be a part of Wimbledon history. It's a big relief because there was pressure from all sides, especially from myself, to do better in Slams".

CHAPTER TWO: GRAND SLAM 2

AUSTRALIAN OPEN 2004

There are always trials and tribulations that an athlete must pass. In 2004, Federer proved to be that amazing player from the previous year. It was even more so when you look at what he managed to achieve in that year.

In 2004 Federer won 11 titles. These included three Grand Slam titles, three ATP Masters titles, and the Tennis Masters Cup. Federer's win-loss record for the 2004 season was 74–6, which was the best winning percentage of any player since Ivan Lendl was 74–6 in 1986.

It was a fantastic year for him. Yet, it should be noted that in that year, he didn't manage to win the French Open tournament. On the other hand, as far as the match-ups and the quality of matches he played, these were extraordinary.

The first Grand Slam he won that year was over Marat Safin, a legendary man who would further propel Federer's undefeatable image. But, before the Marat Safin wins, there were other exciting matches for Federer.

That year Federer played on all possible types of courts from clay and grass to hard courts. It was the all year round achievement, and he was determined to make the most out of it and win frequently. Additionally, 2004 helped him achieve a new image and gain extensive experience, which would serve him in the later years. Right here, on those courts, he would win and build a base not only for future confidence but also for his playing style. Of course, this playful style Federer uses today wasn't formed at once. It took not only a lot of practice but also a lot of playing to develop his style.

Federer entered the Australian Open as the second seed behind Andy Roddick. The Australian Open that year looked rather promising. It was a shark-tank of talent, as many champions were either looking to return to their graces or achieve new heights in their careers. For Federer, it was a special moment since he was looking for that second victory. When you have such a situation on your hands, it's a do or die moment for any athlete. There are tournaments where there's a moment of luck. A big competitor gets injured, or loses in a high-scale game, gets tired and loses against the underdog. But tennis isn't a sport where such things happen often. Instead, you can accept that there are going to be relevant players in the appropriate tournaments.

Winning another Grand Slam was a big moment for his career, and if achieved, it was a sure premonition of something greater. First, it was clear proof that his victory wasn't a matter of luck. Second, if he managed to win another Grand Slam, it certainly was proof that there was a bright future in the sport for him. From the beginning of the tournament, there was a big question of whom Federer was going to face. Star participants like Roddick, Safin, and Hewitt, were almost all players Federer had previously encountered. Strategy wise, it wasn't a good situation. Giving it all against a star player would mean that he would either lose early on or get exhausted and might not be in the top form later in the competition. Here, Roddick and Safin were the greatest adversaries. Roddick lost in 2003 against Federer, and Safin was returning from a long break.

From an initial match set up between Federer and Hewitt, the game seemed to go the way of Hewitt, with 7 wins out of 9 encounters. However, victory did come quickly for Federer, as he had 18 wins against Hewitt's 9 wins. As later matches would prove, the combination of skills and techniques was simply too much for Hewitt. The next match was a more suspense-filled one. Federer met with David Nalbandian, a player he had a prior history with during their previous meetings, Federer lost five of six of their previous meetings. Tempered as Federer is, he couldn't let it go. As usual, it was a suspense-filled game between the rivals. Federer had a lot of problems playing against Nalbandian. However, it was a tight match that Federer barely won.

The next match against Juan Carlos Ferrero was much, much easier. Even though Fererro was ranked No. 3 at the time, Federer dispatched him with ease. The interesting thing about Federer was that he easily dispatched players that were high in the ranking. There are a few theories on why Federer played so well against ranked players early on in his career. One such reason is that they underestimated him. Due to his appearance and lack of experience, it seemed like they could defeat him with ease. Yet, he countered with an arsenal of techniques. Another theory implies that he presented a new breed of player. This new breed commanded different aspects of the game. However, it's more likely that it's the second reason. Later on, critics would credit Federer with a versatile style. The thing most people in sports struggle with is a one-dimensional approach to the game. It's rare for players like Federer to appear. Yet, whether Federer's talent or Safin's experience would prevail remained to be seen. And, thus came a match that was promising to be a critical bout.

The match between Safin and Federer was long-awaited. Safin had an amazing come up in the tournament, dispatching Roddick, among others. It was an excellent match for Safin. A lot was on the stake for Safin in this match. He was returning after a long break, caused by a lot of injuries. The primary injury he had was one of the back, and the lesser one influenced his stamina and leg power. Yet, he chose to return to the pro world.

However, he wasn't without problems entering that match. The thing Federer's camp feared the most was the hunger Safin was coming with. Federer's camp didn't include a coach, just his closest people who followed him that year. Safin did have a previous injury, which made him stay out of the court for some time. But, he also had more experience than Federer, which could be an essential part of such an important match. In most sports, experience has a much more significant role than talent. A young talented player doesn't know the ins and outs of such a high-stakes game. It's easy to lose simply from the lack of understanding of basic things that experienced players know like the back of their hand. However, Federer was still fresh from his victory, and he still had a glow from 2003. He entered the game smoothly and confidently. Disappointedly for many, and luckily for Federer, the match ended in a little over two hours.

Safin had a gambit to play. He did come out strong, defeated Roddick, and entered the finals before Federer. However, the question was whether or not he was ready for the long haul. The injury and time out of the court did something to Safin. Whether he knew he was done before the match or not remains unknown. When Safin entered the game, he didn't look weak or tired. He had a subtle glow and was ready to dominate the less-experienced Federer.

The experience and style should have helped him beat Federer in early sets and keep pressuring him into submission. Yet, that plan failed. Federer proved to be a tough opponent, and he kept fighting in the early sets. While Safin had the upper hand at first, Safin started to lose his composure. His serve's strength was getting weaker, his speed lessened, and his coordination dulled.

Soon, it was evident that Safin couldn't continue and that his legs were done. He had stamina, but his legs and back couldn't take it. It's not known whether he was fully recuperated from his injuries or not. However, it was apparent he couldn't handle Federer. Soon after that, Safin succumbed, and Federer won another trophy. In a short amount of time, Federer was raising another golden trophy. The rest was history.

SUMMARY:

- Final: beat Marat Safin 7-6(3) 6-4 6-2
- Games won/lost: 137/ 74
- Sets lost: 2
- Total time on the court: 13 hours
- Top 10 opponents defeated: Juan Carlos Ferrero (3), David Nalbandian (8)
- Coach: None

- Federer said: "My game feels natural. I feel like I'm living the game out there. I feel when a guy is going to hit the ball, I know exactly with the angles and the spins. I just feel that I've got that figured out. That is just a huge advantage".

CHAPTER THREE: GRAND SLAM 3

WIMBLEDON 2004

I t's a blessing in disguise to have challenges in life. Especially in sports, there are those times when top athletes are pitted against each other. Then, not only do the observers get to enjoy matches of utmost enjoyment and value. But, the players also get to have a confirmation of their true level.

These matches inspire great rivalries. Pitted against each other, these players create amazing games, because it means the world for both of them to win. For the audience, it's just a few hours of complete excitement. However, for players, it's a much different thing. They are forced to play another level because losing isn't an option. Winning means more than a trophy because losing means admitting that there's always going to be better than you.

This year would be incredible for Federer, but it didn't look like that from the get-go. It certainly wasn't like that when he met Andy Roddick for the finals of Wimbledon in 2004. Players had a prior history and would continue to do so in the years to come. Yet, as it's only right, it didn't look like that from the start. The year was already looking promising for Federer. However, beating Marat Safin, who had several injuries and a long break from the professional competition, was one thing. Beating Andy Roddick again was another thing.

Andy Roddick wasn't an unknown player or a player that went up and down on the official rankings. He was a player well-known for his strong shots that made other tennis players tremble. Additionally, Andy had a lot more experience. A year earlier, he was beaten to a pulp, but it was a loss that he shrugged off. But, now, it wasn't something he took lightly. Now, it was real, and Andy Roddick didn't plan to lose. But, if there's a factor that helps make a sports match epic, then it is a great rivalry. And, there's nothing like a young and up-and-coming player beating an already established player. The audience gets a treatment of the lifetime, but players get to see what they are made of.

Coming to the match, Federer already had an amazing season. He was going to win three Grand Slams that year, and the only thing stopping him on that path was his rival Roddick. Rivalry in tennis is different. It's not like in soccer where you have whole teams of people trying to push to perform complex strategies and win. This is personal in every sense of the word. Tennis players have clear aims, which are presented in forms of various trophies, that they want to achieve. Climbing there, obtaining these victories is all these people work for. And sometimes, there's a hand of fate that interrupts in the way of things. It was exactly like that on that day at Wimbledon in 2004.

And remember, this isn't the current era Federer. He didn't have such a sophisticated playing style back then. Also, he didn't have a coach that year, so he was forced to make it independently. He could only rely on himself and his talents only. Roddick already had a defined playing style, which included strong and powerful hits. And, it was believed by critics that Roddick had the upper hand early in the game.

Both players had so much at stake. Roddick had to win this. Losing again against young Federer wasn't an option. Especially since he already lost to him a year earlier. However, the same could be said for Federer. He was on the rise, and winning a Grand Slam would boost his confidence without belief. Comparing his situation earlier with the critics, and drawing an analogy from it, leads to the following point. Do something once and, maybe, it's sheer luck. Do it twice, and nobody can question it. For Federer, that was the situation at hand. At the beginning of the match, it didn't look like he had anything more to offer than a crazy stroke of luck. It was a gray day. Looking at the clouds, it was evident that the storm was coming. Still, Federer was losing the first set. As the critics predicted, Roddick had an easier time getting into the rhythm. Federer couldn't keep up with his strong shots, and Roddick's experience helped him prevail. Federer was getting desperate to turn the tide. And help came in the form of a gray cloud.

The first bad thing happened for Roddick. The match had to pause for the rain to pass. Roddick got into a rhythm, firing his signature power shots. Federer had a lot of problems working those out. And, like it was a godsend, a rain fell. The most significant problem an older player faces when playing with a younger player is one of stamina. When an older player faces a younger player, he wants to wrap up the match early. The longer it takes, the higher are the chances to lose. The younger player may lack experience and skill, but naturally has more stamina and willingness to go for a long haul. Thus, in tennis, establishing dominance is more than necessary for an older player to win.

It was a special moment in Federer's career. Not known to many, but during 2004 he didn't have a coach. Just imagine the pressure he felt. Young, already won a Grand Slam, chasing new victories and new trophies, and nobody to mentor him. He sat in his locker room. Like the year before, when he had a back issue, he had a choice to make. Give it all and win, or fold and lose to Roddick, additionally, losing the Grand Slam. Nobody knew what happened in the locker room that day, but when he returned to the game, he made history.

And that's the point of sports in general. Nobody knows when that moment comes when you can see the player change. They come out, as if they had almost a spiritual change, and start playing like never before. It's even more significant when somebody does it on sheer willpower, without a coach or external advisor. Returning to the court after the delay, transformed Federer.

Looking back to that Grand Slam and Federer's career, it was a time he hadn't won a major US tournament. Also, he still didn't build up that kind of confidence he would have in his other incarnations, years later. But there's something about Federer. It's not his athletic prowess, his unbelievable talent, or the array of techniques he possesses. It's his passion that allows him to win when he needs the most. From another point of view, things weren't looking great for Roddick. He lost his rhythm, and he needed to build up again.

After the rain passed, players entered the court again. Right here, Federer picked up the pace from the get-go. Every service, every backhand and forehand slide naturally, and was morphing into a point. Roddick had significant troubles trying to get back into the game. Even though it was brief, the time off from the court took the blood out of his muscles, making him slower. He couldn't move or use his famous hitting to score against Federer. Slowly, it was becoming more and more evident that Federer was going to win. Yet, Roddick proved to be a formidable opponent. Tensions were running high, but in each set, Federer was coming on top.

Federer came hungry and willing to win. He won. In the excruciating and long game, cut and changed by the rain, Federer won. The entire match lasted for 12 hours and 33 minutes. But Federer's game with Roddick lasted 1 hour and 59 minutes. After all that time, half a day of running, hitting, and stressing, the game finally ended.

Federer got his hands on a second Grand Slam trophy that year and third overall trophy in his life. Andy Roddick had to face a loss from the young player for the second time in his life. He wasn't aware at the time, but it was the beginning of his decline, Nadal and Djokovic would later fortify that. Yet, for Federer, it meant the beginning of an amazing journey.

Even though he didn't win at the French Open, this was the second Grand Slam he won this year. With the second Grand Slam trophy under his belt, he was ready to go three for three. There was another tournament that year, another Grand Slam. It was time to win and enter history.

SUMMARY:

- Final: beat Andy Roddick 4-6 7-5 7-6(3) 6-4
- Games won/lost: 141/78

- Sets lost: 2
- Total time on the court: 12 hours 33 minutes
- Top 10 opponents defeated: Andy Roddick (2), Lleyton Hewitt (10)
- Coach: None
- Federer said: "In the beginning of my career I had a bad record in finals, but for quite a long period of time now I've been winning a lot of them. It seems like I can get my act together at the right time and even stay calm in finals".

CHAPTER FOUR: GRAND SLAM 4

US OPEN 2004

The moment of truth came in the US Open in 2004. After the first win at the Australian Open, and then Wimbledon, the facts were visible to everyone. If Federer were to win another Grand Slam, something that hadn't happened since 1998, he would be a legend. So, the question here had a historical dimension. If Federer were to win this tournament, he wouldn't just be a fantastic young player. He would also be a person that made history.

Everybody knew that Federer was a promising player who would be a relevant player for years to come. His talent, skills, and tenacity were the real deal. Especially after the last match with Roddick, his talent was undeniable. But, the critics are always on the run to question young players looking to achieve stardom and amazing results. But, critics and journalists exist to raise those doubts which make the sport all the more enjoyable. Yet, nobody won the three Grand Slams in a row. It was up to the young prodigy to make it so.

For Federer, it was even more crucial than just three Grand Slams in the same year. Before 2004 he never won a tournament on American soil. In the world of tennis, achieving trophies on multiple continents is a matter of prestige. Therefore, winning is all the more critical since the quality of the tennis player and his ranking get a considerable boost. So, each tournament and win helps the player become the desired No. 1 in the world. For most, it is all that matters in the end, and especially so for a young player like Federer.

If he could do that, it was an unmistakable premonition of the things to come, like those that would happen a few years later in 2006 and 2007. Yet, it wasn't obvious that he was just going to win. Hewitt did lose a few times before facing Federer. To be honest, it wasn't apparent that Hewitt was going to be his opponent in the finals. Like with any other tournament, it consisted of several different participants. So, people were giving Federer the benefit of the doubt. Maybe he could make history, and perhaps he couldn't.

And that's why people love players like Federer. They make them not believe in miracles, but understand that hard work, passion, and determination can lead a man to the pinnacle of life. Additionally, Federer didn't have a coach for the year. It was all him, all the accomplishments and trophies were his effort and his work. So, everyone expected him to come with crazy preparation and an even tougher attitude. Well, it wasn't exactly like that.

Federer came to America in high spirits. He was in peak form, both mentally and physically. Later on, he would admit that he didn't feel especially inclined towards this particular tournament. Additionally, he would lounge in New York and even visited two Broadway shows with his fiancee. His preparation and training wasn't anything different from other tournaments in the same year. He didn't do anything special regarding his approach to training or strategy.

Truth to be told, he already had a win against Hewitt, who he would later meet in the tournament finals. But, as with any other pro tennis tournaments, there were upsets. The young Federer, while looking phenomenal, looked as someone maybe not ready to tackle Hewitt. Federer already made several upsets. He defeated several strong opponents previously that year, and it looked like he didn't have any steam left. After playing a few high-class games, it would be only natural that he didn't have enough strength for another Grand Slam victory.

Hewitt came strong and played against other skilled players with stunning scores, and even more marvelous games. Hewitt was one of the older players, at least compared to Federer. After a few losses that year, Hewitt was looking to enter another tournament to win. He already had established himself in the sport as a force to be reckoned with. He played aggressively and continued stringing victories until he reached finals.

Looking at Hewitt from this perspective, he looked like someone going to beat Federer if he was to reach finals. With all of the evidence presented, critics couldn't disagree that Hewitt wanted to win more than Federer. But, that simply wasn't fair to Federer.

To get a good idea of Federer's rise to glory, you have to look at the lineup of players he defeated before Hewitt. He would go on to play the likes of Albert Costa, Marcos Baghdatis, Fabrice Santoro, Andrei Pavel, Andre Agassi, and Tim Henman before meeting Lleyton Hewitt in the finals. Actually, aside from prying eyes, Federer did manage to win against a group of outstanding players. Yet, all those wins weren't hard-earned like earlier that year. They were achieved with relative ease, which made him all the less interesting. However, as he progressed, it was evident that the chance for writing history was close at hand.

Meeting Hewitt again raised concerns that Federer didn't have it in him. Going against a more experienced Hewitt, especially after he already lost to Federer once, made Hewitt look even more fierce than before. Also, with a gap in experience between them, and Hewitt getting to know Federer's playing style, it looked like Hewitt had this one in the bag. Yet, sports are sports for a reason, and an upset could come from any side at any time.

However, this wasn't Federer from the beginning of 2004. If 2003 was the year Federer was born as a pro, the first two Grand Slams were the event he learned to walk as this new person. Yet, the US Open is the formative tournament of his career. Looking back at his career, 2003 was the year he was still struggling. He would go on to play without a coach; he experienced back problems and played against major players for the first time. There were challenges before him, where he had to make up his mind and decided where he wants to be in his career.

In 2004 he would go on and still have these troubles connected to his confidence. Defeating Roddick a few months earlier could also be considered luck since the rain delay helped him regain composure and win. From the start, Roddick and Federer never had that long lasting rivalry. But it was the second time Federer would defeat Roddick. To some, Federer was just a rising sensation that wouldn't last so long. But he has proved his worth every step of the way.

Yet, this was it, Federer's right of passage. Winning another Grand Slam means that he was born to be a champion, and reign as one for some time. After that point, those five years of struggle would have their true meaning. He would finally be a champion he dreamt of becoming since he was a child.

On the day of the Hewitt matchup, Federer looked inexplicably calm. He entered the field with that special aura he previously had in the Australian Open. From the start, everything went superb. He dominated Hewitt from the first set.

Hewitt didn't have troubles that Roddick experienced. He came in the game strong, looking to win those early sets and dominate the game. Yet, even with previous victories, it looked like Hewitt couldn't do anything to steer the game in his favor. No matter how strong a serve Hewitt had, Federer would counter it.

Federer came out as a sure favorite. Along with the game, he did lose a couple of points here and there, but it didn't faze him at all. He continued dominating Hewitt and ended the game in about two hours.

The more the game progressed, the more it seemed like Hewitt couldn't do anything. Federer would later admit to the press that at some moments, he doubted that what was happening was even real. Every move he made brought him closer to victory. And, everything he did was so effortless. So, he continued pushing, and in less than three hours, victory was inevitable.

And, thus, history was made. Later that day, Federer would hold another trophy, and he would write his name in sport's history by becoming one of those who won three Grand Slam titles in a single year. From that point on, nothing was the same for him. This would be just the first of many years where Federer would truly shine. After all was said and done, one thing couldn't be denied to him. He became a part of the sport's history, and he was there to stay.

SUMMARY:

- Final: beat Lleyton Hewitt 6-0 7-6(3) 6-0
- Games won/lost: 123/74 (Had fourth-round walkover against Andrei Pavel)
- Sets lost: 3
- Total time on the court: 12 hours 40 minutes
- Top 10 opponents defeated: Lleyton Hewitt (5), Tim Henman (6), Andre Agassi (7)
- Coach: None
- Federer said: "I'm very happy with the way I played all tournament. Not even in my wildest dreams would I have ever thought that I was going to win the US Open. Honestly. Now that I've done it, it's still tough to believe".

CHAPTER FIVE: GRAND SLAM 5

WIMBLEDON 2005

Without a doubt, 2004 was an incredible year for Federer. While 2004 marked many of his exploits, 2005 was even better. Before entering the tournaments in 2005, Federer needed some time to recuperate. It was a moment to honestly think about what he was going to do later in his career. So, the next logical step was entering Wimbledon.

During this tournament, he would meet with now standing rivals. From this point on, he would become an active part of the tennis world. However, he would also forge a relationship with other professional players. He wouldn't be just this young, talented player, but also someone they had to acknowledge.

Yet, Federer took his career even more seriously than before. He hired a new coach and a great one at that. He hired Tony Roche to help him improve his technique and develop a style more similar to one he uses today. He was ready for a new pro season full of victories. And, little did he know, it was going to do just that.

The Wimbledon 2005 was nothing short of a shark tank filled with fantastic players, upcoming and veterans alike. Wherever you turned, you could see either a rising star of the sport or a player who had already made a name for himself. Wimbledon 2005 would also mark the first time Federer, Djokovic, and Nadal would compete in the main draw. Aside from them, there were other amazing players, including Hewitt, Ferrero, Gonzalez, and Roddick. Observing this tournament from another player's point of view, this Grand Slam would make sure that Federer and a new generation of tennis players were here to stay. Both Hewitt and Roddick had to admit that after Wimbledon 2005, there were players who they couldn't beat. The shift of generations was apparent, and all who still doubted Federer would meet an unpleasant surprise.

In the initial games, Federer had no trouble advancing to the further stages of the tournament. During this period, Federer was at full strength and capacity. Additionally, with Tony Roche steering the wheel, it was the final nudge he needed for a perfect play. All those little things that he needed to improve on, now were fixed. This only strengthened his ability to win, and execute various strategies and stratagems against unsuspecting opponents.

It would be hard to call it so, but the first upset came in the Gonzalez match. Gonzalez had a lot of trouble dealing with the young thunder in the form of Federer. He outplayed him and outmatched him at every corner. The power that Federer was previously lacking he now found. The critics were usually commenting on Federer's lack of power in his serves and return strikes. Yet, after winning a couple of Grands Slams, Feder would improve upon this weakness and get significantly more potent in all aspects of his games. After that, he would come to play Hewitt again.

Hewitt and Federer would play another match, this time in semi-finals. This would be a second time Hewitt would try to play Federer fully prepared and ready to defeat him. Yet, as people later found out, Hewitt was coming with a lot of pressure on this match. After losing a couple of times to Federer already, the psychological pressure was high on Hewitt. Playing against stronger and younger Federer, after already losing to him in the finals, was strenuous. Looking at him, Federer was up and coming in his career, while Hewitt wasn't in that position. So, winning here would be a huge confidence booster for Hewitt, who tried to win the championship like other participants. Unfortunately for him, he couldn't find the right pace to win this match. It seemed like he couldn't do anything to win.

Hewitt would go on to play his all, trying to defeat the young prodigy. It seemed like he had a counter for every play Hewitt would throw at him. In the breaks, the frustration was noticeable in Hewitt's camp. He tried and tried, and yet, even with all those things considered, he couldn't muster up the power to win. With sad admittance, Hewitt would lose the game and mark the beginning of a new era. There are opponents you can't beat when it counts the most, and for Hewitt such an opponent was Federer. It was all set for the finals, where Roddick and Federer would meet again.

The situation was much different than the previous encounter. For example, Roddick had more experience, more drive, and was a far better player than Hewitt was. And, Roddick had more brawn than Hewitt had. Roddick was an astounding champion before Federer's rise. Coming to the finals, he was expected to be a serious contender. At least the bookies and sports journalists alike were sure that they weren't going to give the favor too early to Federer. Everyone expected a tough match in which a veteran player would have a great battle against a young champion who already managed to defeat him.

It was sure that it was going to be a great match, and that's what everyone at Wimbledon that day was coming to get. The weather conditions that day were great to play. Unlike their previous matches, nothing was standing in the way. All that was left for them was to play it out and see who the better player is. Thus, the match started.

By this time, Federer was known for his excellent opening game. He would come out with a flurry of moves, techniques, and strikes that had Roddick at a disadvantage. Roddick tried to play out his position, but he needed time to warm up and prepare for the game later. Observing it from today's perspective, the most significant advantage Federer had was his youth. The unorthodox playing style, coupled with a strong start, ensured that he won those first sets with ease. And, so it was, Federer won the first set with a blazing 6-2. Then, Roddick warmed up and got serious.

The next set would be a much different story. Roddick had an amazingly strong arm, which reflected in his serves. And, he served them to Federer without a doubt. It was a tight set. However, in their previous games, Federer struggled when Roddick would pick up the pace. This would be a significant problem in Federer's early years. He would start strong and had many more problems when the other player would warm up. So, this was the first time in the match Federer had trouble dealing with Roddick. Yet, as Roddick would later recall in his interviews, Federer felt different that day. He felt like a flawless player, someone who just couldn't lose. Everything Roddick would throw at him Federer would return with ease. Thus another set ended with Federer's win.

The next would be no different when it comes to pressure. The game was intense, and Roddick wasn't letting up. It was apparent at that point. This was nothing less and nothing more than a rivalry. Wimbledon was a vital tournament to win, but winning against the other player was much more important, so they gave their hearts and souls in that match. It seemed like Roddick couldn't do anything. Still, both players were getting tired. The match lasted for more than 10 hours already, and even the young Federer wasn't replenishing his stamina. This was Roddick's last chance to win. And, he did all he could.

However, his age would give up on him. Or, Federer was simply better and younger. From this point in time, it's impossible to tell. Even then, Federer came out as a better player, and that was no contest. After another set and almost 14 hours of play, Federer came out victorious. Thus, a stunning moment came into Roddick's career. Federer was no longer some kid he had managed to win against a couple of times. No, he was his true rival from now on.

As Federer raised another trophy, the world couldn't deny him anymore. He was a real champion and managed to dismantle various opponents without many hardships. Roddick told the world that he knew Federer was a real deal. And, from that point on, Federer had nothing more to prove to anyone. He had only one job. And that job was making history. This was just the first step.

SUMMARY:

- Final: beat Andy Roddick 6-2 7-6(2) 6-4
- Games won/lost: 138/85
- Sets lost: 1
- Total time on the court: 13 hours 39 minutes
- Top 10 opponents defeated: Lleyton Hewitt (2), Andy Roddick (4)
- Coach: Tony Roche
- Federer said: "I really played a fantastic match [in the final]. It was maybe the best match I've ever played. It seemed like I was playing flawless. Everything was working".

CHAPTER SIX: GRAND SLAM 6

US OPEN 2005

After defeating Roddick at Wimbledon, Federer was ready for another tournament, and this time it was the US Open. This time he would go and meet other marvelous players only to rise to the top once more. But, before he could get another trophy and another Grand Slam, he needed to win. Thus, he needed to defeat an array of amazing players.

Now, the shadow of doubt that had resided over Federer's early career was lifted. It was obvious to all that he was making tennis history. However, while all present in the sport's world knew he was going to be great, another question popped into everyone's minds. How great was he going to be?

Just like in Robert Frost's poem, there were two paths, two roads before Federer. One led to various thoughts and opinions others had of his playing style and his game. The other belonged to Federer himself, who knew that only the sky was the limit. Yet, to give some space to the critics, it's their job to doubt and raise concerns. Some of them, even rightfully so, believed that this couldn't go on much longer.

Entering another strong tournament, another Grand Slam, looked almost impossible for most of the critics. However, opinions are opinions, and everyone can have one. But deeds, deeds are something else.

Not everyone can achieve them, and it was time again for Federer to prove his worth.

The list of qualifiers was amazingly strong. For example, this Grand Slam included various players that would all become future champions like Novak Djokovic, Andy Murray, Rafael Nadal, and Stan Wawrinka. The shift in generations was already happening, but it wasn't as obvious from that point in time. You can excuse the critics at the time because those things aren't always possible to get right at the moment they are happening.

For Federer, this was already a fantastic season. He claimed 11 titles and 81 out of 85 wins, losing only to Marat Safin, Richard Gasquet, and Rafael Nadal. Those few losses would not stop Federer, and it was evident that he was coming strong. At least, it seemed apparent from the way he played Ivo Minar in the opening round. He would beat him with scores 6-1, 6-1, and 6-1, leaving Minar defeated. Yet, as Federer already gained a lot of Grand Slam experience, he knew that there was more to come. And, just that happened when he met with Fabrice Santoro. Santoro was a sort of magician, troubling Federer, and making him give everything he got. The struggling game ended with scores 7-5, 7-5, 7-6, making this maybe the toughest game Federer played during this Grand Slam. Then, he would play with Rochus and then with Kiefer, which he would win with relative ease. This all seemed like nothing to Federer, as he would win most of these games and sets without breaking a sweat.

The next opponent he would play was Daniel Nalbandian. Even though he had played him earlier, this time Nalbandian proved to be no threat. The match ended relatively early, with Nalbandian losing 6-2, 6-4, 6-1. And, it was pointed out at that time that Federer didn't have much trouble winning in qualifications. Thus, the semi-final phase of the competition was over. Aside from minor inconveniences, Federer moved swiftly and efficiently to the semi-finals. And that was where the trouble started.

It was time to rekindle a rivalry with Lewitt. Or, so it would seem. Yet, Lewitt also lost a couple of times to Federer, and it looked like he had no chance against Federer. Awaiting this match, Federer was at ease. At previous meetings, Federer would defeat him without any significant issues. As a semi-final match, having an opponent that he had the success of beating was the best thing. He knew Lewitt in and out, and it was a proper warmup for Agassi. It's appropriate to call it a warmup. Lewitt gave it all he had in this game. It was an intense game, where Lewitt pushed as far as he could, but he couldn't win. Federer won with the score 6-3, 7-6, 4-6, 6-3. But, in the end, this was as far as Lewitt would go. He lost the match in less than 3 hours. And, thus, the final came.

On one side the legend slayer, young Federer. On the other side, the legend of the game Andre Agassi. Still, they had met previously in various games. But, what made this meeting special was that this was one of the last games Agassi played. So, it was a poetic final. On one side, a career just beginning, and on the other side, one that's ending. So, all was ready for the showdown. The journalist favored Agassi, but mostly since this was going to be his last Grand Slam. However, observing Federer's meteoric push through this tournament, people were majorly agreeing that Federer was going to win this.

From the outset, the usual thing that happens in all of Federer's matches happened. Federer had a great and strong start as he usually had during those years. It was a part of his strategy to push in those first sets as much as he could. Winning that first set would later help him win the whole game. And, there was a formula for winning right there. Older players needed more time to warm up and weren't able to play as well as the younger players in the first set. Yet, that's only when you look at the first set. The upset came in the second set.

The second set was a real upset for Federer. A long time passed since he had such a bad set in the finals. After Agassi warmed up, he gave Federer a hard time. Agassi's experience prevailed, and he managed to derail Federer winning this set 2-6. However, there was still time to turn this around, and Federer won the first set, so there was nothing to worry about. The match continued.

It may sound like a cliche, but Federer is a type of player who gets the most serious when faced against the wall. Agassi played the last Grand Slam of his career, and he was ready to give everything he got into this match. But, so was Federer. The third set opened with a flash. Agassi's pressure was immense. Yet, Federer fought back like a lion. He got into his mode and continued hitting the ball back. And, slowly, step by step, the youth triumphed. It wasn't obvious that it was going to happen like that at the beginning of the set. But, Federer kept pushing, ending the game with a 7-6 score. So, it all came down to the last set. Whether Federer or Agassi won depended on how they played.

And, just like that, Federer decided it with ease. Agassi couldn't do anything to win, as he would later admit to the press. As he would say, there's nothing to do to outplay Federer. His speed, athleticism, technique, were all on another level. Simply, he couldn't do anything that truly counted in that last set. It was the end of his career, but Agassi wasn't disgruntled with the loss. He accepted a new, younger, and stronger generation ready to substitute them and carry on their legend.

As for Federer, he raised another trophy. Recalling this game years later, he would admit that the last match Agassi would play meant more to him than the trophy. It wasn't like he was happy to extinguish a career. For Federer, it was a special moment, a right of passage to share the stage with an amazing player like Agassi. Another successful year was over for Federer, and he ended it with flying colors.

SUMMARY:

- Final: beat Andre Agassi 6-3 2-6 7-6(1) 6-1
- Games won/lost: 144/89
- Sets lost: 3
- Total time on the court: 15 hours 10 minutes
- Top 10 opponents defeated: Lleyton Hewitt (4), Andre Agassi (7)
- Coach: Tony Roche
- Federer said: "Andre [Agassi] is one of the only living legends in tennis. To play him towards the end of his career, with me being on the top of my game, made it really special".

CHAPTER SEVEN: GRAND SLAM 7

AUSTRALIAN OPEN 2006

If there was an amazing year for Federer, it had to be 2006. That year, Federer would win 92 out of 97 matches, lose 4 times to Nadal, and 3 times on clay. However, nothing is like it seems.

Looking back to this particular tournament, it was the first in a while that had Federer truly struggling. He didn't have an amazing run he had in the previous year. In 2005, he would go left and right to dismantle various veterans of the sport. Yet, even with an incredible 2006 season, the beginning of the year wasn't as promising as 2005 seemed. Still, Federer managed to win this Grand Slam, but it wasn't as easy as it previously was.

The batch of players seemed stronger than usual. And, something was also happening with Federer. This was the first time in a while that he wasn't on the top of his game mentally. During that period, he experienced a lot of psychological turmoil. There are many speculations behind this, ranging from his lack of confidence to Federer feeling down for visiting Australia and meeting his late coach's parents, even though he managed to push through. Luckily, Federer had no problems playing the qualifier rounds. Here, he met Istomin, Mayer, Mirnyi, and Haas. Playing qualifiers was no issue for Federer. He defeated Istomin 6-2, 6-3, 6-2, Mayer 6-1, 6-4, 6-0, Mirnyi 6-3, 6-4, 6-3, reaching Haas with ease.

Along with that, the biggest upset in the qualifier came in the match with Haas, where he struggled for the first time. In the game with Haas, Federer played him 6-4, 6-0, 3-6, 4-6, 6-2, losing 2 sets and still winning. This was the first time in the tournament Federer was struggling. That would be something that would move like a shadow over Federer over the remainder of the Grand Slam. People watching the game could see that something was amiss with Federer. It wasn't like his form or training was lacking; this was a form of internal pressure you could see on his face. It wasn't like he had an injury; this was something inside of him. Yet, he managed to move on to the next round of qualifying matches.

The next match Federer would play was with Dayvidenko. Davidenko came in strong, with a lot of pressure and powerful serve. Yet, there's this thing with Federer, which players could never really tell was it a part of a strategy or just a way Federer used to play. Still, Federer won this set with a 6-4 score. Yet, there was something wrong with Federer, and he would lose the next set with 6-3. But, Federer is a player that seeks victory, he's a humble yet passionate player. In the third set, he came in strong and pushed as hard as he could. It was an intense set with the ball flying across the court at high speeds, not letting you pick a winner. However, Federer would come out on top, winning the set with a score of 7-6. Coming out in the last set, it was a do or die situation for both players. Yet, this was a good thing in a way for Federer. While struggling mentally, he was determined to win. After winning Grand Slam titles two years in a row, he wasn't going to lose now, and not there against Dayvidenko. In the last and powerful set, he managed to come out on top with a score of 7-6. This was the hardest match of the tournament, which Federer won with a lot of problems. Yet, as he was leaving the court that day, it seemed like he was changing. His will hardened, and it was perfectly exemplified in his eyes. The only thing greater than the weight of pain is the taste of victory. That's engraved in every champion, and Federer knew that by heart. So, he prepared for the next match

Next, he would go on to meet Kiefer. This match would be a far less strenuous match for Federer. He would come strongly, winning the first set with ease. He had new energy now, and he was dispensing it without concern. As it's common in Federer's matches, he wins the first set with ease. That was perfectly emphasized in the score 6-3, where the opponent had little and almost nothing to offer against Federer. The first set passed without much inconvenience for Federer, as he pushed past all of Kiefer's efforts. Then, the second set came. For a brief moment, Federer was off guard. He lost his focus, and let Kiefer score 5-7 against him. Federer had a few bad serves, and a few returns he couldn't parry. The champion suddenly fell. Observing the last few games he played, it seemed like he wouldn't pull through. Yet, there is something about that early Federer. It seemed like no matter how much adversity he had to go through, he would grit his teeth and win. That, exactly, is the beauty of sports. You don't know what people carry in their souls until their back is up against the wall. And, that's something Federer embodies perfectly. At least, he did it with a score of 6-0 in that set. His eyes were full of that fire once again. Thus came the last game. As he was closer to the finals, you could feel Federer waking up to that powerful player he always was. He won with a staggering 6-2 and ended the match. Finally, it was all set up for him to meet Marcos Baghdatis.

Entering the game, Baghdatis seemed like a strong contender. Before coming to finals, he even defeated Roddick. And, he would later play Ljubicic and Nalbandian. Those were all the players Federer defeated in the past year, some in semi-finals, and some even in finals. However, for Baghdatis, this was a tournament full of excitement. He managed to win all his games with a combination of pressure and effective gameplay. Most importantly, he was coming in a strong contender after defeating Roddick. All that was left was for finalists to meet and determine who was going to be the champion.

Federer didn't look at his best. The turmoil from the previous matches was still there. Everybody could see it. Baghdatis was a different story. He came in strong and started giving Federer trouble from the very beginning of the match. The array of serves, backhands, forehands, and returns dismantled Federer in the first set. He fought and struggled, but it seemed like he couldn't do it. The results of this set were Federer's loss of 5-7. Baghdatis looked powerful, confident, and most of all, he looked like a strong contender. It wasn't looking like Federer was going to do much. This time, people around the court felt the same thing. They felt like Federer's run was coming to an end. Like those last three years didn't mean as much compared to what was happening right now. Federer hadn't lost the first set in a Grand Slam final in a long while. But, that story of invincibility seemed like it was coming to an end.

Yet, in sports and life, there's something called "champion's pride." It's that moment when a champion has to overcome his limits and give all his got to defeat the opponent. It's something that pushes people to do marvelous things, and Federer was a champion. And a champion always has his pride as his greatest weapon.

As Baghdatis would later admit, he underestimated Federer. He saw him crumble in the first set and started to play a more relaxed game. This would cost him dearly. Federer started playing a more aggressive game, picking up the pace and coming out as the winner of that set with a score of 7-5. The next set would be a set of total Federer's domination with a score of 6-0. Now, Federer picked up the pace and showed no sign of any mental vulnerability. He came in this set, stormed it, and set the pace for the final set. So, the last set came, and he defeated the opponent with 6-2. He made history, won another Grand Slam, and unsuspected by all around him, he started crying. Later on, he would admit he played for his late coach, whose family was on the court that day. He raised another trophy in his arms and celebrated the victory. That day, he didn't just defeat a dominant player and won another trophy. That day he also defeated himself, and winning against your vices is the greatest thing any man can do. It was the premise of the things to come.

SUMMARY:

- Final: beat Marcos Baghdatis 5-7 7-5 6-0 6-2
- Games won/lost: 149/88
- Sets lost: 5

- Total time on court: 16 hours 1 minute
- Top 10 opponents defeated: Nikolay Davydenko (5)
- Coach: Tony Roche
- Federer said: "Being such a huge favorite in the final [put a lot of pressure on me]. If I had lost, it would have been the biggest upset since I don't know when. I was incredibly nervous going into it".

CHAPTER EIGHT: GRAND SLAM 8

WIMBLEDON 2006

If there are championships that define the history of sports, then Wimbledon 2006 was one of them. Not only was it a part of an amazing season for both Federer and Nadal, but it also put their rivalry in the spotlight. The most interesting thing about this year's Wimbledon was the build-up to it. Nadal and Federer previously met, with Federer losing to Nadal a couple of times before Wimbledon. Yet, this could be addressed because they were playing on clay courts, hard courts that favored Nadal. Wimbledon was different since it was a grass court, and grass courts were Federer's natural habitat. The year 2006 saw a lot of fantastic players as seeds and qualifiers in the tournament. Who would come to the finals, and who would be the king of grass that year?

After the Australian Open, Federer regained his composure, and as he would later state, he felt like Pacman, eating trophies and tournaments. Yet, even with him winning 91 out of 95 games that year, there were 3 losses to the young Spaniard. Something was brewing behind the scenes, and everybody knew what it was. Looking back at 2003, nobody could anticipate what would happen in just a few years later. The situation was almost identical, and now all of the lights were right in Nadal's face. The only question here was the following. Would

Federer reign as the king of grass, and would Nadal be the one to dethrone him?

Yet, the mental fatigue that plagued Federer in the Australian Open was nowhere to be seen. It was a different set up for him. He fully regained composure and, entering the tournament, it was obvious that he was gunning for the trophy. Coming into the game, he would face various opponents, winning almost every set from the beginning of the championship to its end. There were some upsets, but they were almost too few to mention. Also, some critics claimed that he had some luck with the draft, as he was passing stronger players, and getting more favorable picks for his ascension in the tournament. However, that remains questioned, since all those stronger players were the players Federer won against previously. In the known tennis world, it was evident that there aren't many players who could upset Federer aside from Nadal.

For example, the first opponent he met was Gasquet. Federer had already played against him and ensured a victory before. Unlike the Australian Open, Federer was dominating from the very start of the match. He beat him with scores of 6-3, 6-2, and 6-2. Though Gasquet was a great contender, he couldn't do too much against the sharp and dominant Federer. The next few matches were almost identical to this one.

The next opponent he would face was Henman. Henman was a great player, and yet this was nothing for Federer. Though, it was an admittedly hard first set for Federer. Henman put on the pressure in that set, trying to force Federer as much as he could. Still, he lost the set, and the game continued. The next set was even worse for Henman, where he lost utterly. Federer picked up the pace, and Henman couldn't do anything to stop him. The match ended soon after that, ending the game with the scores of 6-4, 6-0, 6-2.

Following the match with Henman, Federer would meet with Mahut next, which he would go on to dismantle with the scores of 6-3, 7-6, and 6-4. After that, he would play Berdych, which he also demolished with the scores of 6-3, 6-3, and 6-4. This wasn't a big ordeal for Federer, who was ready, prepared, conditioned, and, most importantly, mentally prepared to play this as best as possible. In the minds of critics, journalists, and people around the court, it was apparent Federer was coming to the finals. And even more so, the players he was facing knew that this was Federer who wasn't going to buckle down like in the Australian Open. Thus, the moment came for him to face Ancic.

Ancic put on a show and played as best as he could. Yet, Federer overplayed him in every possible way. Anicic tried to put pressure on Federer as much as possible. It was an obvious strategy that all players tried to utilize. And, the whole strategy rested on the player's ability to put as much pressure in the first set as possible. If they could take that advantage, maybe there was a way to defeat him in the next few sets. Well, it wasn't a strategy that worked out great for Ancic anyway. Björkman was the next player Federer would face.

Yet, even the champion of doubles such as Björkman couldn't do much against Federer. Björkman tried his best, but he served as a warmup at best. Even the game's score was tragic for Björkman, as he lost to Federer with the scores of 6-2, 6-0, 6-2. Thus the game ended, and everything was set for the finals. As many predicted, it was the time for the showdown of two promising young players. It was time for Federer and Nadal to face off against each other. It was, in a way, something that everybody wished to see. While Federer was winning his games, Nadal was winning his.

Nadal came in strong that year. For him, winning against Federer would mean more than just going home with a trophy. Like Federer was on his run to become the best player in the world, so was Nadal. And Nadal had another advantage over Federer - he was the younger guy in the match. Therefore, he was in the same position Federer was three years ago. He wanted to win big tournaments, beat legendary opponents, and become the greatest that ever was. To add to the injury at Federer's expense, Nadal managed to beat him three times already.

But this was different. Federer is the king of grass, and Nadal was a promising king of clay. Each player had his favorite terrain, and both Federer and Nadal tried to adapt to all terrains. There's something from those early days since tennis players pick up the racket for the first time. It's something in their blood. So, there was a psychological incentive for both Federer and Nadal to win. If Federer was to lose here, he had to acknowledge that there's a younger player who already outmatched him as he did to the veterans. However, if Nadal were to lose, he had to recognize that there was still a ways to go and that for the rest of his career, he would have to overcome a considerable obstacle called Federer. Thus, the finals began.

The first set came as a disappointment for many. Nadal lost the first set with a score of 6-0. It looked like Nadal had nothing to offer and that the course of the match was set. However, Federer made a crucial mistake here, which wasn't usual for his gaming style. He relaxed, and he dropped his guard.

Nadal capitalized on that, and played a rough second set, pushing Federer to the limit. Still, he lost another set to Federer, with a tight score of 7-6 for Federer. Yet, Federer couldn't release at all; it was obvious that Nadal was going to push and give his best to dismantle him at this point. Nadal pushed through in the next set, and each time he hit the ball, he was coming on top. Hit by a hit, return after return, he managed to come on top and win the set against Federer with a score of 7-6 for him.

However, Federer didn't want to loosen up there; there was too much at stake. Thus, Federer pushed as much as possible. Federer started to apply pressure even further. Nadal, even as a prodigy as he is, couldn't do almost anything against Federer. He lost the set with 6-3. Finally, Federer could breathe and relax. He was victorious. Nadal had to admit his time was yet to come. Federer was still young and strong, and as promising as Nadal himself was. However, that day something else happened. A new rivalry was born, and it was carved in stone for tennis history. A relationship that the tennis world so desperately wanted had finally arrived.

SUMMARY:

- Final: beat Rafael Nadal 6-0 7-6(5) 6-7(2) 6-3
- Games won/lost: 134/68
- Sets lost: 1
- Total time on court: 12 hours 9 minutes

- Top 10 opponents defeated: Rafael Nadal (2), Mario Ancic (10)
- Coach: Tony Roche
- Federer said: "I'm very well aware of how important this final was for me. If I lose, [Rafa] wins the French and Wimbledon back-to-back. I was twice in the final. It was important for me to win a final against him for a change".

CHAPTER NINE: GRAND SLAM 9

US OPEN 2006

Sports have a great thing about them. They come with a drama that's unrivaled even when you compare it to television and films. In some tournaments, new players come, and nobody suspects they are going to be future champions. They come and play, and maybe even do nothing special to impress the audience. On the other hand, there are those moments that define the end of a player's career. When you combine all that in a single tournament, you get the exact reason why people love sports so much. The US Open 2006 Grand Slam was precisely that. It brought the excitement people waited for. And, it was a unique situation for Federer as well.

It was even more for Federer. After beating Nadal at Wimbledon the same year, it became even more critical to win more Grand Slams, more championships, and more tournaments. That, of course, doesn't make Federer greedy. On the contrary, it's a part of sportsmanship to try to win as many trophies as you can. And, Federer was attempting to do just that.

Additionally, the trophy means, even more, the better the player becomes. That was the situation he was dealing with. Yet, talking from a spectator or a historian's point of view is easy. The hard thing is to predict who is going to win now. Even more so, it's harder actually to win the tournament when you are the person participating.

From the very start, the US Open that year had many strong contenders. Among them were the greats that Federer played earlier like Agassi, Roddick, Lewitt, Blake, Davydenko, Baghdadis, and others. Yet there were up-and-coming players like Nadal and Djokovic who were both participating. Of course, the rest of the pick was just as amazing. Yet, not all of them were destined and made to be champions. As for Federer, he was in peak condition. Aside from the Australian Open, where he wasn't entirely mentally ready, this was a completely different situation. That year, he already won two Grand Slams, and he was prepared to win another.

The tournament started as usual for Federer. Aside from a Fernandez game a few tournaments earlier, there weren't any incidents that stopped or upset Federer in any way. In the first game, he met with Jimmy Wang, who he defeated with a score of 6-4, 6-1, 6-0. And it wasn't anything special for Federer. Usually, during those first matches, Federer would meet opponents that weren't able to play on his level. It seemed like it was never a question of whether or not he would pass to the higher stages. It was just the question when it would happen.

In the next match, Federer would meet with Henman, who he also previously beat. There, the gap between the new and old players was visible. Federer's generation came with a variety of techniques, and they are more versatile than the old generation. Naturally, that doesn't mean that they are worse than the new player. It's just a thing that happens in every sport. A new generation brings a new freshness to the game, and they get that freshness from learning and transcending their effort and technique. Henman couldn't do much against an opponent he lost previously to in the same position. The game ended with a score of 6-3, 6-4, 7-5. Even though Henman put up a great game, there wasn't much he could do before losing the game.

The next game was a far easier matchup for Federer. He met with Spadea, and it was a much shorter and easier game. Spadea couldn't do much, while Federer was just playing his usual game. The match ended with a score of 6-3, 6-3, 6-0. In these matchups, Federer would advance with ease, and just move through the ranks to the next match. And, his last match before entering the finals was with Gicquel. This was a more pressuring match, but it didn't phase Federer at all. He won the first set easily, while the second set was more interesting. Finally, Federer defeated him with a score of 6-3, 7-6, and 6-3. Thus, Federer was ready for the last part of the tournament.

There, he met James Blake in the first game, which is where things got interesting. Blake wasn't like the previous players. He was the real deal. He'd won championships before and even was a holder of the No. 4 best in the world player. And he was going to give Federer a run for his money. The match was intense from the very start. The usual thing Federer would do is to put a lot of pressure on his opponents, and then try to force their hand as much as possible. Well, that almost didn't work on Blake. Federer barely won that first set with a score of 7-6. However, Federer came out strong and won the second set with an amazing score of 6-0. Blake, even with his amazing flat forehand, couldn't defend against Federer's rush. However, the upset came in the third set, where Federer lost to Blake with a 7-6 score for Blake. The final set was decided with an incredible play from Federer, and thus the final score was 7-6, 6-0, 6-7, 6-4. In the next match, Federer would meet Davydenko.

Davydenko came out as a perfect player to excite Federer for a final. Davydenko had already lost to Federer in a similar situation in the finals. Davydenko couldn't do much against Federer. It is evident from the first set that this was going to be a hard match for him. Federer rushed the first set and beat Davydenko with a 6-1. Davydenko tried to fight in the second set and still didn't win. The set ended with 7-5 for Federer. Davydenko tried to apply pressure but ultimately lost in the third set with the score of 6-4 for Federer. Now, everything was ready for the finals.

Roddick had an amazing run this Grand Slam. He beat many contenders, yet none of them were really upon his level. He went on and defeated them with relative ease, with only a few matches here and there, which were a few upsets. Yet, Roddick played with ease. It was sort of his comeback in the tournament. Almost like Federer, he had a relatively easy uprise to the finals where he met with Federer. Now, this was a different situation than before. Now, they were real rivals, and Roddick wasn't interested in losing.

Thus, they met, and the finals began. In their previous matches, Roddick had the upper hand in those first sets. Roddick would come with his missile service and dominate Federer early on. Federer needed that time to recuperate and pick his pace along the first set. Yet, Federer had a different idea for the first set. He rushed Roddick and put pressure on him before Roddick could compose himself. Federer beat him 6-2. Yet, that was just the first set. The upset came in the second set.

Roddick played a better game and defeated him with a score of 6-4. However, that's where the Federer machine comes in and shows what he's made of. After the tough second set, came another tight set. Here, the game continued at the same pace. However, Federer had a clear advantage by which he played Roddick a couple of times. He'd learned his power, speed, and technique, and it was much easier to counter him this time. And that reflected perfectly in the score of 7-5 for Federer. So, it all came to the last set. However, that's where the true upset came. Federer came in the last set and pushed Roddick to give everything he got. Roddick tried and tried, but he almost couldn't do anything. That reflected in the final set with a score of 6-1 for Federer. Federer raised another trophy, and Roddick couldn't hide that Federer wasn't going to loosen up.

This was Agassi's last tournament and a tournament where Federer's dominance was assured. This was the third US Open in a row for him to win, thus making history. While other players entered the competition directly into the Hall of Fame, others carved their names into that same history. Sports are truly amazing.

SUMMARY:

- Final: beat Andy Roddick 6-2 4-6 7-5 6-1
- Games won/lost: 141/76
- Sets lost: 2
- Total time on court: 13 hours 43 minutes

- Top 10 opponents defeated: Nikolay Davydenko (6), James Blake (7), Andy Roddick (10)
- Coach: Tony Roche
- Federer said: "I feel like I'm the best player of this generation, but nowhere close to feeling the best ever. Just look at the records that some guys have".

CHAPTER TEN: GRAND SLAM 10

AUSTRALIAN OPEN 2007

When you compare all of Federer's previous Grand Slam appearances, something is missing. It isn't a thing connected to the way he plays, not at least with his athleticism, technique, speed, or strength. No, this is different.

This was an experience worthy of a champion. Of course, that wasn't his direct fault. He had to work his way to this position, and just like a rock becomes a diamond, that's how Federer became a champ. If anything, he showed all his power and might and a fantastic strategic mind when he played Roddick. This was an interesting moment in Federer's career. He'd already managed to make history in the sport. However, there's always a question of what a person can do.

That question came to Federer once again in 2007 at the Australian Open. Would he win another time in a row? Was there a chance for him to beat others again and raise the trophy? Interestingly enough, he lost at Kooyong Classic to Roddick, which got Roddick's spirit high. Like any other contestant, it's just as important to Federer as it is to any other player to come in high spirits when approaching such a prestigious tournament.

Looking back at 2006 and 2007, you could say that these were the formative years for many players, especially for the Big Three. The Big Three, which includes Federer, Nadal, and Djokovic, was gaining momentum. Each of the players would create an amazing career from that point. Yet, that may not be the best explanation of what is going to happen, since Federer already established himself as champion. Nadal was just behind him, already beating him in French Open, and all that was left for Djokovic to start winning and rightfully join them. However, there was some time between that point and this time. Therefore, looking at this tournament, you could see that the shift of generations was in full swing. Roddick had a serious problem, and that problem was perfectly personified in Roger Federer. By this time, it was clear that he couldn't beat him until the tournament before the Australian Open. There, a glimmer of hope shined, and it seemed like there was a limit to what Federer could do. Thus, all contestants entered the tournament.

The first match of the tournament had Federer pitted against now-retired player Phau. From the very start, Federer had what could only be defined as a strong game. Even though Phau was seriously fighting back, he managed to push him back and ascertain the victory in the first set with a score of 7-5. After he warmed up, he brought his classic game back to the court. The second set was strong for Federer with nothing to lose and maximum excitement for the audience. He managed to dismantle Phau with a score of 6-0 in the second set. However, the third set came with a pinch of hope that Phau could turn something around, but it was to no avail. He lost the third set to Federer with a score of 6-4 for Federer.

In the next match, he met, once again, with Björkman. He defeated him in an almost identical setting a year ago. Björkman tried to play as good as possible, but Federer was rushing in. He would send powerful serves and strong backhands to win the first set with a score of 6-2. The former champion couldn't do much in the second set. The score of the second set was a bit different, as it ended 6-2. Finally, came the third set without a lot of excitement, since it ended with a score of 6-2.

The next match had Federer pitted against Youzhny. This was a match with a lot more excitement. Still, Youzhny couldn't do much against Federer. Federer dominated the first set with a score of 6-3. The second set ended with an identical score of 6-3, and the play in these two sets was almost identical. The pressure came in the third set, where Youzhny stepped his game up and delivered a fantastic play. Still, it wasn't enough to stop Federer, as he defeated him with a score of 7-6.

Finally, Federer met with Novak Djokovic. Unknown to anyone, this was the beginning of a great rivalry. Later, in the future, they would play many more games where they would battle for the position of No. 1 in the world. However, this was still early Djokovic, and he couldn't do much against Federer at that point in time. Federer bested him in the first set with a score of 6-2. Djokovic returned with a better play in the second set as he came with great gameplay, leaving Federer to win with a score of 7-5. Djokovic still tried to return, but it was to no avail. Federer won the last set with a score of 6-3.

Thus, the finals could begin. In the quarterfinals, Federer would meet with Robredo, a Spanish champion who held the position of No. 5. Here, Federer met with real resistance for the first time. In the first set, Federer came with a rush and asserted dominance over Robredo winning the set with a score of 6-3. Yet, Robredo picked up the game in the second set, pressuring Federer further. However, even with the astounding game Robredo played, it wasn't much he could do to stop Federer, as Federer defeated him with a score of 7-6. Robredo tried to give his best and turn the game around, but he couldn't score in that set. Federer won the set with a score of 7-5 and ended the game.

The game that was more interesting than the final itself was the match between Federer and Roddick. This game perfectly emphasized how complex sports are. There's this moment of brilliant strategy players use that could span over several tournaments. Roddick felt like he finally had an answer for the puzzle that was Federer. His confidence wasn't without reason; he'd finally managed to defeat Federer before the tournament itself. With the new coach, new gameplay, and a brand new win, the journalists and critics waited for the match feverishly. There was this widespread belief that there was something Roddick could do. So, the match came, and everyone was highly anticipating it. However, going to the finals was nothing relevant. Here, the essential thing centered on whether or not Roddick would finally defeat Federer.

The court observers could see that Roddick was coming in strong. The thing engraved in his soul was Federer's rush, a strong play that decided the first set. Even with powerful serves and strong returns, Roddick couldn't beat Federer, and thus Federer won with a score of 6-4.

Then, it finally came. In the second set, Federer came with an upset. Everything Roddick tried to do was meaningless. Federer had a counter for his every move. He obliterated him with a score of 6-0. And, he lost another set with the score of 6-2, finishing the game. Right there, he knew that what he played a few weeks earlier wasn't the real Federer. He let him win on purpose to gauge Roddick's game and defeat him at the tournament. A terrible conclusion came over Roddick. There was nothing to do against Federer. The semi-finals ended, and so did the most anticipated match of the tournament.

The finals were less than exciting, as Federer met with Gonzalez. Now a former pro player, Gonzalez tried to do his best. He came rushing at Federer and tried to apply pressure from the onset. The first set was a tight game, where Federer won with a score of 6-4. Then, the expectations dropped, as Federer would defeat him in another set with a score of 6-4. Finally, Gonzalez tried his best to return to the game, but there was little he could do, as Federer won with a score of 6-4. The tournament ended with a less than exciting finale.

But that's the beauty of sports. It's truly the best man who wins in the end, and Roger proved that he, surely, was the best man.

SUMMARY:

- Final: beat Fernando Gonzalez 7-6(2) 6-4 6-4
- Games won/lost: 132/72
- Sets lost: 0
- Total time on the court: 13 hours 19 minutes
- Top 10 opponents defeated: Tommy Robredo (6), Andy Roddick (7), Fernando Gonzalez (9)

- Coach: Tony Roche
- Federer said: "If somebody had told me that I would win 10 Grand Slams from mid-2003 until today, I never would have thought there was any chance of doing something like that. I would have signed up for just one".

CHAPTER ELEVEN: GRAND SLAM 11

WIMBLEDON 2007

There are amazing moments in sports. These moments are usually born out of rivalry. There is nothing more a sports fan, and an athlete could wish for. A true rivalry pushes the player to unknown heights and ensures that the athlete doesn't yield. It gives everything something to hope for. And, most of all, rivalry creates historic matches that are going to last forever.

Such rivalry is the one between Federer and Nadal. It was just a few years earlier that Federer had all the advantages over Nadal. However, Nadal won many matches against Federer and proved to be a real contender to being the best of the new generation. The problem was, for each player, one of prestige. It was apparent that they were going to have amazing careers, and that they both were going to be historically important players for the history of tennis. But, that is something for the books. It's a different thing to live through those moments. For both, victory is everything. However, only one of them returned home with a trophy. The other becomes second in the competition, and that's simply not good enough. Thus, the Wimbledon of 2007 started.

One thing was clear from the start. Federer was returning as a two-time champion. If he were to win another Wimbledon, he would become the second in history to win three Wimbledons in a row since Bjorn Borg. However, the exciting moment was that Nadal was also about to make history. If he won this tournament, he would become the second in history to break the strange double French Open Wimbledon record. And, also that would be a second time in history that someone would break Borg's record. So, the only thing left to be decided was who was going to advance to the finals and make history.

As always, those things aren't visible from the start. Yet, both the critics and journalists were aware of the possibility of the Federer-Nadal finals. However, it was still too early to say that it was going to be that way since it included a lot of fantastic players.

In the first match of the tournament, Federer played against Gabashvilli. The Russian player was well-known for his strong serve and hard groundstrokes. Still, it was far from enough to stop Federer's rush in the first set. Federer won the first set with a score of 6-3. This affected the Russian's confidence, and he played even worse in the second set with a score of 6-2. Finally, the Russian gave all he got in the final set, but it simply wasn't enough, and Federer won with a score of 6-4.

For the next match up, he met with Potro, who proved to be not much of a challenge for Federer. He came with the usual strong start, defeating Potro with a score of 6-2. Then, Potro returned harder in the second set, playing more aggressively and putting up a fight. He almost defeated Federer in that set, but ultimately lost with the score of 7-5 for Federer. Finally, Federer got the last with ease, beating the Russian with a score of 6-1.

Interestingly enough, he had another match with a Russian player, this time with Safin. Safin was also a No. 1 player during his prime in 2000. However, this time Safin came with a slow start, and he couldn't defend against Federer, who rushed him winning the set with a score of 6-1. In the next set, Safin tried to recuperate, but to no avail, and he still lost the set with a score of 6-4 for Federer. Finally, he played an amazing last set, still unable to win, and losing to Federer with a score of 7-6. From this point on, Federer proceeded to the quarterfinals as he got a walkover against Haas. So, everything was set for him to make history here.

The quarterfinals pitted Federer against Ferrero, one of the players to achieve No. 1 status as well. For Federer, this was a great experience since he was able to play against various high-profile players and defeat them. However, it would do those opponents great injustice to say he walked over them too. On the contrary, this was a great game. The first set was thrilling, and it ended with a score of 7-6 for Federer. In the next set, Ferrero managed to beat Federer with a score of 6-3. Then, Federer got serious and ended the following two sets with the scores of 6-1, and 6-3, defeating the Spaniard.

In the next match, he would meet a player he previously defeated. Playing against Gasquet a year or two earlier was far easier than it was this time. Gasquet played an intense game from the start, pushing Federer to his limits. The first set was the toughest for Federer, but he managed to pull through and win 7-5. After the first set, Gasquet slowed his pace as Federer continued to apply pressure. He defeated him with the scores of 6-3, and 6-4, ending the game and entering the finals. To make things historic, Nadal also entered the finals. History was about to be made.

That's something Bjorn Borg knew, watching the two players enter the court that day. One of his records was going to be obliterated. Yet, nobody knew which one. And, that made things even better.

Nadal had played a great tournament so far. He played against the line-up of players such as Fish, Eschauer, Söderling, and Youzhny. In the quarterfinals, he met with Berdych, and later Djokovic. Even though he lost the first set, he managed to get right back up and defeat Djokovic in two following sets and ensure that he is going to the finals.

Their game was nothing short of spectacular. The tensions were high, and the rivalry was real. They both were hoping to win, as they would make a name for themselves, beat their rival, and make history that day. People around the court, critics, and journalists were in a state of chaos. The very suspense gathered as both players entered the court was immense. However, all those hearts singing together in excitement weren't nearly enough to foreshadow what was beating in the hearts of those two men standing against each other. Thus, the Wimbledon final of 2007 began.

From the onset, the game was very intense. Both players were looking to win, and even more so, both players had a history winning against each other. They knew each other's move, techniques, speed, and strength. Everything was rather high-paced, and the first set ended with Federer's victory with a score of 7-6. The second set picked up right where they left off, and it was full of Nadal's dominance, as he was putting on a show, pressuring Federer and winning with a score of 6-4. Federer had to step his game up, and Nadal wasn't going to let his concentration deteriorate in this crucial moment.

The third set was the continuation of the powerplay of two legendary players in the making. It was a set of fast returns, stronger services, and amazing techniques. Yet, Federer managed to come out on top and defeat Nadal with a score of 7-6. However, the next set was the set of Nadal's dominance, as he defeated Federer with a score of 6-2. It was all left to the final set to decide the game. Right there, Federer pulled everything he got, and defeated Nadal with the stunning result of 6-2, ending the game. Falling to his knees, Federer cried and shouted, unable to hide his true feelings. That day, Federer entered history.

It was an amazing road so far. In just four years, Federer managed to do so much that it was almost impossible for a single person to do. Yet, it was possible, and he made it possible. But, he could also lose to Nadal. That's the price of rivalry, and this time, Federer reaped all the benefits from it. It was an amazing day for Federer and the tennis world alike. Cheers.

SUMMARY:

- Final: beat Rafael Nadal 7-6(7) 4-6 7-6(3) 2-6 6-2
- Games won/lost: 123/70 (Had fourth-round walkover against Tommy Haas)
- Sets lost: 3
- Total time on court: 12 hours 29 minutes
- Top 10 opponents defeated: Rafael Nadal (2)
- Coach: None

- Federer said: "Rafa and I have been at the top for over 100 weeks together. It's building up to maybe one of the great rivalries. You can't always play five-set thrillers, but I'm happy it happened today. I left as the winner. It was perfect".

CHAPTER TWELVE: GRAND SLAM 12

US OPEN 2007

Aside from rivalries in sport, there is another, even more exciting event. That event is when you put another contestant into the game. When you observe the rivalry Feder and Nadal have, it brought many fruits to sports fans worldwide. And, that situation just got way better when Djokovic entered the stage.

Djokovic would become another player whose rivalry with Federer would achieve legendary status. During that period, both Djokovic and Nadal were still very young, with the former being 20 and latter being 21. Federer had a few more years of experience than them, and that did reflect in his game. Yet, even Federer could see that things weren't going to stay the same anymore. It was more than evident that he had the upper hand when playing against veterans. However, there were now two more players who were hungry and passionate enough to usurp his title and stand in these major tournaments. As fate would have it, they would become the Big Three of the sport. However, it was still too early to talk about that, and these were Federer's golden years. He was on a run a lot of players can only dream.

Since defeating Lewit for the first US Open title in his career, Federer always felt high confidence. Something felt natural for him, and he had every right and reason to do so. He had just made history after breaking Borg's record. There were greater things for him. Aside from Nadal, he couldn't see anyone who could stop him, or usurp his standing as the greatest player of his era. Thus, the US Open of 2007 began.

His first opponent was Jenkins. Jenkins had an overall standing of No. 18 on the ATP list and wasn't a strong contender for Federer. This reflected on the results as Federer dominated the entire game. He bested Jenkins with the outcome of 6-3, 6-2, and 6-4. Unlike other tournaments where Federer usually has a bit of a slow start, he was rushing and winning this game with ease.

In the next match, he played against Capdeville, who proved even easier than the previous opponent. The game wasn't a thrilling experience, as Federer dominated his opponent. The score reflected that perfectly as the first set ended with a score of 6-1. Capdeville tried to force Federer's hand in the next two sets. However, it wasn't enough to stop him, as Federer ended the next two sets with a score of 6-4.

Yet, the casual nature of the first two matches would come to bite Federer back as he faced Isner. The bad thing about Federer in those early years of his professional career was that he would sometimes lose focus due to relaxation. Isner capitalized on that perfectly. Also, he achieved No. 8 on the ATP list and was famous for having the strongest serve in his era. That powerful serve helped him best Federer in the first set with a score of 7-6. Even though Federer did lose the first set, it wasn't something that affected Federer negatively. It was a positive thing since he bested Isner in the next three sets, where Federer would beat him with a score of 6-2, 6-4, and 6-2.

In the fourth round, he played Lopez, whose highest rank on the ATP list was No. 12. Federer couldn't warm up in the first set and lost the set with a score of 6-3. Yet, as Djokovic would later praise him, he has an astounding mental toughness. He can move through anything and come out victorious. That was precisely the case when he beat Lopez in the next three sets with a score of 6-4, 6-1, and 6-4. Now, he was ready to enter the quarterfinals.

In the quarterfinals, he met with Roddick, who now had a history of losses against Federer. It just happens that way sometimes. Sports are ruthless, and today's champ may lose tomorrow like he never was the best to grace the court. Such was the relationship between Roddick and Federer. Federer came in strong and usurped the place Roddick held for so long. And, they were facing each other once again.

However, Roddick was more than ready to face Federer. Both players gave everything they got, but Federer came out on top once again. The fierce first set ended with a score of 7-6 for Federer. It was a tight set and a warning of battle to come. The second set was almost identical; it was a high-level play that ended with a score of 7-6. After losing the second set, Roddick deflated and lost the game's final set with a score of 6-2.

In the semi-finals, Federer met with Dayvidenko. Looking back at his games, Dayvidenko was never a strong contender against Federer. He never beat him in the finals and wasn't going to do so again. Federer came in strong and played an amazing game where he won 7-5, 6-1, 7-5. And, everything was set for the finals where he would meet Djokovic.

At the Wimbledon that happened the same year, Djokovic lost to Nadal. However, this time Djokovic had a bunch of tough games that led him straight to the finals. He played against Haase, Štepanek, Potro, Monaco, and then against Moya, and Ferrer. In all honesty, he didn't have an easy match, and unlike Federer, he didn't have opponents that he just ran over. However, after beating Ferrer, the 20-year old Djokovic was more than ready to take on Federer. And, taught well by his experience with Nadal, Federer knew better than to underestimate Djokovic. As players entered the court for the finals, it's unknown whether or not Federer knew that Djokovic would be his second rival.

Either way, the finals started. It was a tight game from the very start. Federer tried to rush the young Djokovic, but it was to no avail. Djokovic returned with a strong game, employing everything in his arsenal to beat Federer. Yet, Federer managed to beat him in the first set with a score of 7-6. The second set wasn't anything less than an amazing thrill to watch. They continued playing with the same intensity, with the ball flying back and forth between the players. The intensity of the game didn't let up, not even for a second. However, there were a lot of things Federer would capitalize on.

Djokovic made a lot of mistakes, losing points and losing sets for marginal errors. He made some rookie mistakes, which led to Federer winning. Aside from that, Federer would lose points when his focus would shift, and he let Djokovic earn easy points from him. Yet, that didn't change the second set, which ended with a score of 7-6.

Thus, came the last where Djokovic was still trying to turn the game around. However, he couldn't make it. Federer defeated him with a score of 6-4. So, another Wimbledon ended, and Federer won his straight, fourth Wimbledon title.

However, while it was a sweet victory, it wasn't a perfect one. His win against Djokovic wasn't easy, and Federer started to wonder about the future. It was apparent to him that things weren't going to be so easy from now on. Instead, he was going to play against two opponents who were going to become even better. And he came to a fascinating point of his career. After a few years of an amazing run, he now faced the situation players he defeated faced when he came into the game.

He dismantled legends left and right, but now, the other two players were doing the same thing he did. It wasn't like he was going to get any younger, or they any worse. Nadal already proved that he could win against Federer, and it was only a matter of time when Federer was going to do so.

Thus, it all ended. There was no doubt in anyone's mind that things aren't going to stay the same any longer. Victories, sometimes, are sweet. On other occasions, it may be just a step away from a loss. However, nobody thought about that, as the celebration went on.

SUMMARY:

- Final: beat Novak Djokovic 7-6(4) 7-6(2) 6-4
- Games won/lost: 141/89
- Sets lost: 2
- Total time on the court: 12 hours 54 minutes
- Top 10 opponents defeated: Novak Djokovic (3), Nikolay Davydenko (4), Andy Roddick (5)

- Coach: None
- Federer said: "I've enjoyed the challenge of young guys challenging me. This is probably my biggest motivation out there – seeing them challenge me, beating them in the final. It's really for me the best feeling".

CHAPTER THIRTEEN: GRAND SLAM 13

US OPEN 2008

When you look at any professional athlete's career, there are ups and downs. And, no matter how you look at it, there are moments when they have to fail. Maybe, it's an appearance of a new contender that shakes the era. And, sometimes it's an injury that puts the player out of commission. However, sometimes there are occurrences when all kinds of different aspects happen and push greater players back into the fold, stripping them of their grace.

Such a season came in 2008 for Federer. The warning of many critics who waited for Federer's downfall came true in two different tournaments. At the Australian Open, he lost to Djokovic in the semifinals. The loss came as a shock to Federer, who relived the scene he had with Nadal. It certainly was impossible for him to continue winning forever. However, the loss came at a bad time when he was looking to make history and further push his career. Then came the French Open, where he lost to Nadal. Nadal managed to dismantle him on the court, where Federer had the least success of playing against him. To top it all, Federer had an injury. It looked like his run was finally ending. Yet, before losing two Open tournaments, there was another one that Federer continued for years, and that was the US Open 2008.

He returned as a champion to the US Open. Yet, there were a lot of doubts concerning his comeback. After the injury and two major losses, it seemed like Federer's run was finally ending. Still, that's where the athlete's spirit shines the most. It's an amazing moment when one loses and has to dispel the doubts and lack of confidence only to win again. However, the Big Three were in full swing. They were becoming equal. As Djokovic already defeated him once, it wasn't impossible to do so again in the future. But a champion is always a champion. His true worth is shown where he is summoned to defend his title. The US Open was a Grand Slam Federer where he felt like he was at home. And, he rightfully did.

The qualifying matches were rather usual for Federer. For him, it was completely normal to dominate the qualifier. And he did so when he played against Gonzalez. He pushed through the first match and asserted dominance from the first set, winning with a score of 6-3. After warming up, he had another marvelous set where he won with a score of 6-0. The final set saw another spectacular game from Federer when he won with a score of 6-3.

In the next match, Federer would meet with Alves. That game was a bit harder for Federer, where he felt more pressure from Alves than he did against the previous opponent. Although the game got more complicated, Federer still won the first set with a score of 6-3. After that, Alves applied more pressure where he pushed Federer, but it simply wasn't enough. He lost to Federer, who won with a score of 7-5. The whole game ended in the third set, where he won with a score of 6-4. The crowds were hyped about the return of the champion, but there were still ways to go.

For his next opponent, Federer had Štepanek. Štepanek didn't prove to be much of the challenge either. He defeated Štepanek in three sets, where he pushed the opponent in all sets. The game ended soon, as he defeated Štepanek with the score of 6-3, 6-3, and 6-2. There was only one match left for Federer before advancing to the finals.

In the last qualifier match, he met Andreev. After a series of wins, he encountered his first real threat. He played against him, but this match was something far different than what he usually experienced in the qualifying matches. The game was intense from the start with Andreev winning the first set with a score of 7-6. Federer played a tight game, but it was time to get serious.

The next set had a more serious Federer that started pushing back. The champion's pride was kicking in, and he began scoring points left and right. He defeated Andreev in this set with a score of 7-6. Federer played another set, now with more fortitude and more elegance. He managed to take another set with a score of 6-3. However, the game came with an upset in the fourth set. Andreev managed to turn the game around and beat Federer in the fourth set with the score of 6-3. It all rested on the final set. The champion wasn't letting up, and he pushed, defeating the opponent with 6-3 in an exhilarating last set.

Everything seemed fine. In the next match, he played against Müller. Müller played a fine game, but that was all there was to it. He didn't manage to do anything significant against Federer. Federer won the game with a score of 7-6, 6-4, and 7-6. Then, came the Djokovic match.

In their last meeting, Djokovic defeated Federer in the semi-finals. Federer wasn't going to let that happen again. The champion's pride was kicking in. When a player reaches that point in their career where he already establishes himself, he doesn't need the beginner player's motivation. Instead, the achievement itself becomes his pride and his motivation. And, nothing in the sports world is greater at motivating people than a rivalry. Nothing pushes the man as far as rivalry can. So the match commenced.

Federer started playing in his usual strong fashion. It allowed him to dominate Djokovic in that first set, winning the game with a score of 6-3. However, Djokovic had a plan of his own and returned with an even stronger pace in the second set. He pushed Federer even further, beating him with a score of 7-5. However, Federer didn't want to let up here. He couldn't afford to lose another game against Djokovic this far into the tournament. Federer channeled all his experience and skill to beat him in the third set with a score of 5-7. Finally, after the fourth set, he could rest for a bit, where he defeated Djokovic with a decisive set with a score of 6-2.

Another thing that went great for Federer was that the other finalist, Murray, defeated Nadal in the semi-final game. Meeting Nadal could be disastrous as he already beat him previously that year. Murray wasn't somebody Federer played often, and that was just what he needed. Yet, Federer didn't despair. He was glowing. He came back to defend the title, and rightfully so.

Murray had a great run on his own, with Nadal being the best player he faced. Yet again, Murray had an amazing career already. He was just as hungry to win the title as the next guy. Maybe Nadal wasn't playing against him in the finals, but that didn't release him from the fact he was playing against a fantastic player. Thus, the match commenced.

Federer came in strong and defeated Murray with a score of 6-2. That alone wasn't a reason for celebration. Murray returned with an even fiercer game than before, pushing Federer to his limits. Even then, Murray couldn't beat Federer as he lost to him with a score of 7-5 for Federer. In the final set, Federer defeated Murray with a standing result of 6-2. Thus, Federer made another historic win, staying undefeated for five straight years at the US Open tournament.

And that is the story of a champion's pride. There's nothing more significant than it. Each year, new players are coming into the game. They have a lot of heart, motivation, and a lot of wins to win. But, a champion has his reputation, which is his pride. He doesn't want to lose because the loss is an emotional event for him. He wants to win because the champion status is a part of his status, it's a part of the sport, and it's a part of history.

Even though Federer is an extremely humble athlete, he's not immune to it. No matter how you turn it around, it was a journey of blood, sweat, and tears to get to that position. Federer, being the great player he is, wasn't going to let it all go. And, that's why he's the best of all times. He had the guts to pull through.

SUMMARY:

- Final: beat <u>Andy Murray</u> 6-2 7-5 6-2
- Games won/lost: 146/91

- Sets lost: 3
- Total time on the court: 15 hours 42 minutes
- Top 10 opponents defeated: Novak Djokovic (3), Andy Murray (6)
- Coach: Jose Higueras and Severin Luthi
- Federer said: "I came in with good spirits from the Olympic Games. I guess I stayed in that cloud and just kept it going here. I actually beat some really good players in tough conditions, and the relief was enormous".

CHAPTER FOURTEEN: GRAND SLAM 14

FRENCH OPEN 2009

Another fascinating thing about sports is that dreams do come true. If there's a way to show that hard work can make any dream true, then that way is in sports. There is nothing like that moment when an athlete manages to achieve his goals after a lifetime of unyielding battles. When you add rivalries and injuries into the mix, the win becomes even sweeter.

Tennis is exceptional precisely for that. No matter how special a player is, there's the moment of the terrain or the court they are playing at. Federer earned the nickname King of Grass because of his superiority when playing on the grass. However, that's the exact reason the French Open was such an unachievable goal for him. He played on it, alright. Yet, the problem here was that the clay had its king too, and that king was Rafa Nadal. Nadal defeated him on at least three different occasions, reigning as the King of Clay. It was a wound in the back of Federer's mind. He was only a single ATP tournament win away from breaking Sampras record, and engraving his name in the hall of fame forever. Yet, with Nadal and Djokovic on the rise, it was rather tough just to keep winning. Along with that, Federer had an injury, and 2008 wasn't his best year.

But, here's the thing about hard work no one can deny. It's those solemn, silent moments, where an athlete gives everything he has to train. It's hours and hours of practice, hours and hours of sacrifice, and years of dreaming and having those dreams broken. And yet, it's to rise again, to dream again, to play again, with the faint hope that you will raise that trophy that eluded you for so long. That wound, in Federer's life, was the French Open tournament. Still, Federer is a champion, and a champion never gives up. So, after a bad 2008, Federer entered the French Open.

The greatest threat, of course, was the match with the champion Nadal. He had a historically bad play against him on this type of court. If he had to meet him again, the probability was high that he would lose against him. But, that's the beauty of sports, they are so unpredictable.

In the first match, Federer met with Martin. Federer's standard play in the qualifying matches had the usual combination of a strong opening set, followed with a pressure in the next two sets. Martin wasn't going to do much, and Federer defeated him with ease. Aside from the first set, where Martin put on a show, he didn't do much else, as Federer won with the scores of 6-4, 6-3, 6-2. While that game could be deemed uneventful, the second game was different.

In the next match, Federer met with Acasuso. This already proved to be a tough match for Federer, since his opponent had awesome serves, and favored clay. It was apparent that it was going to be an intense match right from the start. Federer barely won with a score of 7-6. Yet, that meant almost nothing in the second set. Acasuso stepped up his game, pushed Federer, and made him uncomfortable. Federer succumbed to the pressure, losing the set with the score 7-5 to Acasuso. Yet, Federer wasn't giving up, he played with even more fervor, and managed to win a tight score of 7-6. In the end, he managed to win a score of 6-2.

Now, Federer was ready for the second match. He met with Mathieu. Right off the bat, he lost the first set. Yet, he kept his composure and continued playing. He returned in the second set and managed to win. Surprisingly, that was the only upset he had in this match and won the rest of the game with scores of 6-4, 6-1, 6-4, and 6-4. Then, he met with Thomas Haas.

Thomas Haas gave Federer a walk over a few years ago at the same moment as the tournament. Well, he wasn't going to do that again. He came in strong and beat Federer in the two first sets with the score 7-6, 7-5. The game didn't look bright for Federer. The last thing he needed was to be defeated at this stage of the tournament. He couldn't have that. Not now or ever. Relying on everything he had gone through, training, wins, and losses, he put everything in and pushed forward. He managed to get back and win the third set with the score of 6-4. By the fourth set, Federer seemed revived and dominated with a score of 6-0. It was all to be decided in the final set, where Federer came in victorious with a score of 6-2. Now, Federer had reached the finals.

Yet, even though those early matches were hard enough, something amazing happened. Nadal lost to Söderling even before reaching the quarterfinals. Without the champion in the mix anymore, it was highly possible to win the French Open for the first time in his career. The biggest obstacle had been removed. Any player could win the tournament now, and Federer wasn't letting go of the chance of a lifetime.

In the first match of the finals, he met with Monfils, who was at his best, ranked No. 6 on the ATP list. However, Federer was on the run, and he wasn't letting up for even a second. Federer came in strong in the first set and defeated him, winning the set with a score of 7-6. With the dominance now assured, Federer slid through the game scoring 6-2, and 6-4 in the next two sets.

However, the biggest upset game came in the semi-finals. Clay was killing Federer, literally killing him. He met Potro, and things were far from looking great. He immediately lost the set with a score of 6-3 for Potro. Then, Federer recuperated in the next set with a score of 6-2. Yet, Federer wasn't letting up. He came back strong and won the next set with a score of 6-1. It was all to be decided in the fifth set. Federer came in rushing and won with a score of 6-4. All that was left was to win in the final match, and Nadal was nowhere to be seen.

To make this even better, his opponent was the one who put Nadal out of commission. It was a do or die moment. All that separated Federer from the title was that one small victory, one victory in the finals. Let's get it.

Federer came in rushing. He played a perfect first set defeating his opponent with a score of 6-1. The second set was far more problematic as his opponent was doing everything in his power to win. He tried and tried, but still couldn't do much as Federer would win the tight set with a score of 7-6. The victory was at hand. The set started, and Federer was playing like his life was on the line. He pushed and applied pressure, and the moment came. He won the last set with a score of 6-4.

He fell to his knees, and tears came flowing from his eyes. After all those years of the French Open eluding him, he finally won, he finally got the trophy. And as you can see, that's why hard work pays off.

All the struggle, all the losses, it meant nothing at that moment. After all those years of struggling, he finally managed to win. There's nothing like a victory, and nothing means more than a victory hard-earned. Federer earned it that day and achieved history. He made Sampra's record, but before anything else, he bested himself. The problematic clay surface was finally overcome. In his eyes, he had finally become a true champion.

That's all that's important in the end. It's not all about winning; it's about the journey that makes it happen. There are no caps on dreams, and whether you are a pro player or a regular guy, making your dreams come true is everything in life. Go on and do it.

SUMMARY:

- Final: beat Robin Soderling 6-1 7-6(1) 6-4
- Games won/lost: 156/111
- Sets lost: 6
- Total time on the court: 18 hours 35 minutes
- Top 10 opponents defeated: Juan Martin del Potro (5), Gael Monfils (10)
- Coach: Severin Luthi

- Federer said: "It's maybe my greatest victory, or certainly the one that removes the most pressure off my shoulders. Until the end of my career, I can now play with my mind at peace and no longer hear that I've never won Roland Garros".

CHAPTER FIFTEEN: GRAND SLAM 15

WIMBLEDON 2009

After winning the French Open, Federer entered Wimbledon. Yet, nobody knew what was going to happen at the Grand Slam that year. After witnessing what happened at the French Open, everybody expected that Federer was right back to where he was in 2007. However, things were getting even more interesting when Federer entered Wimbledon in 2009. This Wimbledon tournament would lead Federer to yet another epic match, with another rival.

This time he would play against Roddick again. Yet, Roddick would come out after a lot of time and try to defeat Federer. Unlike their previous encounters, Roddick came with a concrete strategy, fierce spirit, and tough gameplay to face Federer. Their rivalry, which already was epic, was getting a grand finale.

The best part was, you can't know these things when the tournament is starting. And, that's why people love sports. They can't anticipate what will happen, making the experience all the more amazing.

In the first game, he met with Randy. Federer had a strong start, and he defeated Randy with a score of 7-5, 6-3, 6-2. The game had the first set with high intensity, which later diminished in the two latter sets, where Federer dominated.

In the next match, Federer would meet with a Spaniard, Garcia Lopez. From the get-go, Federer dominated the game. Garcia Lopez couldn't do much against Federer. Federer rushed the Spaniard, and applied the pressure, winning the first two sets with ease. He won with a score of 6-2, 6-2, leaving the third test with a score of 6-4.

The next match pitted Federer against Kohlschreiber, who gave a high-intensity game for Federer. Federer dominated the first two sets with relative ease. He won with a score of 6-3 and 6-2. However, the upset came in the third set when Kohlschreiber returned and won the set. The set was rather intense, and Federer lost by a margin. Yet, he didn't slip. He defeated him in the following set. It's something typical for Federer. He often regains composure after losing a set, and that's perfectly reflected in the score of 6-1, with which he ended the game and passed to the next match.

SUMMARY:

- Final: beat Andy Roddick 5-7 7-6(6) 7-6(5) 3-6 16-14
- Games won/lost: 159/114
- Sets lost: 3
- Total time on court: 15 hours 47 minutes
- Top 10 opponents defeated: Andy Roddick (6)
- Coach: Severin Luthi
- Federer said: "I'm happy I broke [Pete Sampras' record of 14 Grand Slam titles] here because this is always the tournament that's meant the most to me. It definitely feels like it's come full circle for me".

CHAPTER SIXTEEN: GRAND SLAM 16

AUSTRALIAN OPEN 2010

Every competition comes with its challenges, but Federer wastes no time in going for the win. Immediately after his chain of victories at Wimbledon 2009, Federer set foot on Australian Open 2010 soil. The Open 2010 marks the 98th edition of the event, and it appears it has become a recurring decimal for Federer to take home the title. The event is the first Grand Slam of 2010.

Committed to his craft as always, Federer brought dark clouds into Andy Murray's skies, defeating his dreams of a win. Federer pulled a 6-3 6-4 7-6 (11) win at Melbourne to claim the victory against Murray at the Rod Laver Arena. Federer was in no mood to relinquish the 16th major title to anyone, not Rafael Nadal, not Andy Murray.

Defending champion Rafael Nadal lost out of the game at quarter-finals against Andy Murray. But Andy's victory didn't come without a fiercely contested battle with Nadal. It appears that age, health issues, and more, all favored a win for Murray as Nadal's quadriceps injury forced him to retire from the singles competition early. Then entered the world's best, Roger Federer, who went for Andy's jugular at the men's competition with a solid win.

Federer's journey to the Australian Open 2010 made it the seventh Grand Slam finals back-to-back. He had earlier won two out of three initial men's competitions at the 2009 Wimbledon and 2009 Roland Garros. His preparations and agility pay off every time.

For many, the Australian Open was an emotion-laden one. Federer came on board with no plans to take on any prisoner. As the world watched, Andy Murray represented great hope for Britain, an opportunity to clinch the major title since Fred Perry's Grand Slam victory in the US Open of 1936. But Federer's preparedness and skills was an uphill task for Murray. Meaning the Brit's 74 years of waiting for a Grand Slam singles win continues unabated.

As he lost at the second Grand Slam finals against the Swiss giant, Murray apologized to the British audience over his inability to clinch the championship with teary eyes. "Sorry, I couldn't do it for you tonight," Murray reported having said when facing a cheering crowd.

It was an emotionally tense game. Though Andy Murray put up a good fight, Federer was all set for the win. Murray admitted it would require his best performance against Federer to secure a win at the finals. But his opponent was far too prepared for a win to allow the match to go against Federer.

The last two Australian opens achieved similar emotional responses from Federer. In previous opens, Federer openly appeared low when he lost in the final five sets. But this year, Federer's excitement knew no bounds as it was the fourth championship held at Melbourne, and he was determined to secure a slot at the 16th Grand Slam. Federer said, "All of a sudden, it was over, and it hit me: It was very much a roller-coaster."

This victory places Federer as the first dad to emerge the winner of major singles within the space of seven years back. He said, "I m over the moon winning this again. I played some of the best tennis in my life these two weeks. It's also very special - the first Grand Slam as a father."

In the 2009 open season, Federer's loss to Rafael Nadal came about when he was soon to become a father of twins. A devastated Federer broke down due to Rafael's defeat. The champ was almost in tears when making his presentation to the public. But in 2010, Federer found his voice. This time the tables were turned against Murray as he said, "I can cry like Roger... It's just a shame I can't play like him."

Federer took control of the game, delivering every shot to precision. Not that Murray displayed any sign of being an inexperienced player, but Federer's flowing style and attacks left Murray with limited options to go for a win. At the end of the game, it was evident that Federer had weathered the storm to retain his position as the greatest tennis player of all time.

Federer and Murray entered the finals with high hopes. For Federer, he placed his confidence in his wealth of experience, plus he had a comfortable win against the Scottish player during the 2008 US Open Grand Slam finals. US Open 2008 resulted in six wins for Murray against Federer's ten. Therefore, Murray hoped to bridge the gap this time and go for a possible victory by raising the bar in the Australia Open 2010.

Yes, the odds seemed stacked against Murray, but he didn't betray it when he took his first opening shot. Murray made a firm and nicely struck backhand serve to commence his second Grand Slam finals. For Federer, this was his 22nd finals, and he came through with consistency and experience.

Initially, Murray was content with maintaining a steady flow of action as the game built up. But Federer suddenly launched an offensive going all the way with a forehand and backhand strike to tip the game to the 2-0 side. Murray was agile and equally swift. He is not one to take things lying down. Just as was the case a fortnight at Melbourne, Murray made moves for a quick recovery.

Federer was not one to bulge so quickly. Instead, he made a counter volley which gave Murray a narrow opportunity to pounce, firing a backhand to the rear line. The shot went out of the court but earned Murray two breakpoints, which he converted in a brilliant show of sportsmanship, making an equal forehand shot that headed to the opposite flank.

At one point, the game was in favor of Murray. He made some impressive but long shot baseline rallies with constant changes in pace, causing Federer to be almost everywhere at the same time. Things began looking up for the Scottish sports giant, a win looked likely. But the Swiss sports giant, Federer had three narrow but well-taken chances. The chances plus some impressive serving helped

Federer get away with three additional breaking points in the fifth game.

As the competition became intense, Federer's prowess at the game gradually became more evident. His brilliance was at its peak. Federer made a historic backhand stroke down the line and immediately followed it up with an unmistakable and undetected forehand to earn a 5-3 lead. Federer was not yet done with his moves as he served his set with consistency and ease.

One of the challenges Murray experienced was that he consistently served at a 45% giving slimmer chances of rallying cheap points. It also gave Federer a better opportunity to control and return Murray's serve with ease. Federer made a break again immediately, and the second set commenced. Without delays, he hid a cross-court at a forehand to clinch the winning shot.

Federer was excited and in top gear at this point, and there was little Murray could do to stop the Swiss sports giant. The winners kept zipping past Murray while he did a great job avoiding a double-break at the rear. In game four, Murray managed to adopt a backhand winner to ace his chances and ended with a 15-40. Federer kept the onslaught going on a near-deflated Murray.

Federer brought game six to an end at 30-30. The odds were stacked against Murray, who, although he made four impressive breaking point saves in preceding games, started experiencing slight issues with his thigh. There was so little Murray could do to stop Federer. Thus, Federer took control of the serve to advance into a two-set lead, which only worsened Murray's position as he had to make the fight from the bottom.

However, he is not one to give up quickly and not in the middle of an on-going fight. But it didn't take long to work up his emotions. In game two, Murray smashed up his racquet after he missed a backhand at the breakpoint. He, fortunately, saved the situation by striking a quick forehand to result in a 4-2 clear. For Murray, the good news ended in a tie-break but not without so many pent up emotions and dramatic displays.

In the case of Murray, he missed a chance to convert points from five sets on two occasions. Those points should have earned him a win.

Federer also missed two match points. The first occurred over a forehand pass that went wide out of position. Federer's second miss came after he unwittingly allowed Murray's shot to float past his racquet to settle at the baseline.

Overall, the tension lasted about two hours and 41 minutes before Federer brought the game to a halt. He got a deserving victory after Murray erroneously placed his backhand into the net. Murray fought hard and put up a good fight.

Close to tears, Murray congratulated Federer for a well-deserved victory. "I'd like to congratulate Roger. His achievements in tennis are incredible. To keep doing it year after year is pretty special. He was much better than me tonight so well done to him for that".

Federer admitted that it was a closely contested match and appreciated every step of the competition. "Ändy, well done for your incredible tournament. You're too good a player not to win a Grand Slam, so don't worry about it."

About his victory, Federer said, "I'm over the moon winning this again. I played some of the best tennis again of my life these last two weeks".

Federer was now a proud dad of two lovely twin girls, and he took to traveling with his family while defending his title.

SUMMARY:

- Final: Federer defeated Andy Murray - 6-3 6-4 7-6 (11)
- 98th Edition
- Games Won: 135
- Games Lost: 74
- Sets: 3
- Sets lost: 2
- Total time on the court: 14 hours 53 minutes
- Top 10 opponents defeated: Andy Murray (5), Nikolay Vladimirovich Davydenko (6), Jo-Wilfred Tsonga (10)
- Coach: Paul Annacone

CHAPTER SEVENTEEN: GRAND SLAM 17

WIMBLEDON 2012

The Wimbledon 2012 sporting year was another exciting one for Roger Federer as he emerged the winner of the Men's Single 2012. The Grand Slam 17 victory placed Federer again at the Number 1 position in the world. This victory turns out to be Federer's seventeenth Grand Slam tennis title and the seventh Wimbledon title ever.

Federer had to defeat defending champion, Novak Djokovic, to make it to the finals against Andy Murray. Because of this victory, Federer became the first tennis champion to make an appearance at the single's finals eight times.

Again, Andy Murray had to come face to face with the world champion, Roger Federer, for a scintillating and fierce battle. For the Scottish, this was not going to be like other years because he was determined to go home to Britton with a win this time. Remember, it was 74 years back in 1936 that the Britons held the title last with Fred Perry clinching the victory during the US Open.

At 24, Murray wasn't too young for a win as others have achieved the same feat at an earlier age. The likes of America tennis player, Micheal Chang, at age 17 became the youngest player ever to win the

Grand Slam singles Open and became the number 1 in the world in 1989. However, for Wimbledon men single victories, Boris Becker holds the title for Grand Slam wins. Boris, at the age of 17 years, defeated Kevin Curren to lift the title. Currently, Rogers Federer still retains the title.

For Federer, anything short of another victory was not conceivable. Finally, the competition ended 4-6, 7-5, 6-3, 6-4 in favor of the world No. 3 player to attain No. 1. Therefore, Federer said, "I was almost shocked the moment that it all came together so nicely." But what transpired? The intrigues, errors and mistakes, high points, and more at Wimbledon 2012 make up the discussions in this chapter.

"When I won in 2003, never in my wildest dreams did I ever think I would win Wimbledon and have my kids seeing me lift the trophy," says Federer. Thus the competition was an important one for Federer. At least, if nothing else, the joy of fatherhood and having his lovely twins present at the stands was enough for Federer.

Although, things were beginning to look up for Murray, even though Federer was approaching the peak of his career. Federer, however, was able to pull the steam to ensure the winning streak continued. Federer's back injury didn't make the competition an easy one. Right from the third-round game against Julien Benneteau he had to nurse an injury but was able to manage it into the finals. He managed so well, he took Novak Djokovic, intercepting a lightning strike at the semi-final match.

The Wimbledon 2012 title was a fiercely contested one. Though Federer took home the title, Murray kept getting better at each set. Each win was with tears of joy for Federer but also showed the die-hard spirit Murray possessed. The energetic, young, and hungry player, Murray, looked like he was going to be around for a long time.

If Federer claimed the victory at Wimbledon 2012 he would move from being No. 3 to No.1. The event also placed him as the record holder for the most weeks ranked at the tournament, emerging World No. 1. It was a position held last by Pete Sampras. This victory came just a few months before his 31st birthday. However, in some quarters, many stacked the odds against Federer winning the competition. But again, Federer took on Murray like he has done on several occasions and in the Australian 2010 Open to record another victory.

While Murray did everything possible to avoid the first four defeats at the finals, Federer was gunning for another win. Murray was yet to secure a single major win or title. This year's event would mark the third title contest between Federer and Murray. Federer won the other two finals at US Open 2008 and Australian Open 2010, which made Murray more agitated for a win.

The 126th edition of the tournament took place at the Grass Courts, England Lawn Tennis, and Croquet Club at Wimbledon, England. Federer had earlier defeated Djokovic at the semi-final to secure a ticket for the finals. Murray made history by being the first British player to get to the Wimbledon singles final for the male category at the Opens.

The finals started on a low note. Both players were still testing the waters and trying to get their groove going but at a steady pace. Things began to get heated up such that even the eventual victor wouldn't find it an easy victory. Murray had garnered much experience and also attained the World No. 1 status. Federer had lost some ground in the past two years but was still a potential threat.

To give him the Wimbledon 2012 victory, Federer had to ensure his serves were consistent. His backhand, forehand slice, and netplay were some of the intrigues that would guarantee the much-expected victory. He initiated his best serves to such jaw-dropping precision with each hit and at every corner. In some instances, Federer displaced Murray with such brilliancy, a deeper wealth of experience, and masterly strokes even at the start of each serve. Some serves were unsuspected moves.

Roger Federer's wealth of experience in the field is an unprecedented one. However, Murray is not less of an experienced player as he made equally impressive serves that caught Federer unguarded. On other occasions, he brilliantly picked Federer's serves and returned with remarkable backhands or forehand to place Federer in an awkward position. At some points, he had a temporary loss of focus. But that should be expected considering that he is playing against a more experienced Federer.

In the first set of the finals, Andy Murray made it clear he was not there to play as he made an early win against Federer with a 6-4 victory.

Set two was a more heated game where Murray fought to keep the second set on a positive note for him. Federer had a little difficulty securing an early win. But with sheer determination and skill, Federer leveled the game with an eventual win at 7-5.

As for the third set, it provided an equal avenue for Federer to continue his winning spree. Roger started with a two-set to one ahead of Murray in the finals.

Set four of the competition resulted in a 6-4 win for Federer again. His magical serves, front and backhands and points added up to give Federer the victory. It all went down within a four-set to provide Federer with the victory.

Through the game, Spanish umpire Enric Molina ensured both contenders stayed within the rules or enforced discipline. Considering the tenseness and importance of the game, that's the least that the game deserves.

To put the game into full gear, both players traded breaks until Murray gave Federer a break during the ninth game. Murray's serves, therefore, resulted in 6-4 points. However, due to some slight misjudgment, Murray lost some impressive chances to have placed him on good standing during the second set giving Federer a lead with the four breakpoints.

Federer took on a further lead when he released a volley winner to set point, breaking Murray at 6-5. Although it had never happened in Wimbledon's final history, the skies seemed to be in a mood for celebration as it suddenly began to rain during the third set. Therefore, it forced the management to suspend the competition and shut the roof for about 30 minutes.

When they resumed, the game entered its critical moment during the sixth game. The third set lasted for about 20 minutes and produced ten deuces. Federer took advantage of some rare opportunities at the sixth break to make a win.

With a clear opportunity in the fourth set, Federer made a break from his serving to finally secure his 17th Grand Slam title and seventh Wimbledon championship. While Federer celebrated his victory with a kiss of the trophy, runner up Murray had to face the fourth defeat at the Grand Slam. However, barely a month after, Murray claimed his victory over Federer with a three-set straight win at the Olympic Men's single in 2012. Murray got a gold medal representing Great Britain in the Olympics at Wimbledon, England.

However, Murray had better seasons coming for him as he became victorious at the US Open when he secured his first Grand Slam title in 2012. He also acquired his first Wimbledon title in 2013.

His historical performance places Federer's seventh win in the class of Pete Sampras's victory of 286 weeks in 1936. He broke Sampras's records on July 12, 2012. Thus, Federer became the first Britton after Fred Perry to lift the trophy at 4-6 7-5 6-3 6-4 at the Centre Court, England.

However, the whole game had a virile set up right from the start. When Lukas Rosol of Czech encountered Rafael Nadal in five sets, it created an avenue for Federer to make the run for the title. From the competition, Nadal made a head-to-head win exceeding Federer by 18-10 but leading at 8-2 for the Grand Slam play. Over the year, Nadal had defeated Federer twice at the Wimbledon finals.

Nadal posed a significant threat to Federer in the course of the competition, but all thanks to Rosol, who eliminated Nadal early enough. In all, Federer's 17th Grand Slam title didn't come cheap but was well deserved. As the sports giant gradually approached the twilight of his career, he still insisted he was not done yet but coming on stronger.

SUMMARY:

- Final: Federer defeated Andy Murray - 4-6 7-5 6-3 6-4
- 126th Edition
- Games Won: 150
- Games Lost: 86

- Sets lost: 5
- Total time on the court: 15 hours 33 minutes
- Top 10 opponents defeated: Andy Murray (4), Novak Djokovic (1)
- Coach: Paul Annacone and Severin Luthi

CHAPTER EIGHTEEN: GRAND SLAM 18

AUSTRALIAN OPEN 2017

C all him the tennis wizard, and you won't be so far from the truth. How Roger Federer maneuvers his way to somehow clinch the 18th Grand Slam title of the Australian Open 2017 is still worthy of note. In no small feat, Roger Federer took on arch-rival Rafael Nadal in the men's Australian Open finals at the Rod Laver Arena to emerge victoriously.

The event lasted three hours and 37 minutes, a victory that made Federer one of the oldest ever to win the title at age 35. He holds the second position to 37 years old Ken Rosewall in the Australian Open 1972. Federer defeated 30-year-old Rafael Nadal by 6-4, 3-6, 6-1, 3-6, 6-3, although it took Federer ten years to beat Nadal at the Grand slam.

Notable for being very emotional, Federer shed some tears when he thought about the uneasy victory. Going through five sets against Nadal? That couldn't have come as an easy victory, added to the fact that Federer just came out of six months of a knee injury. He, at one point, broke down in the fifth set. Yes, Federer had defeated Nadal 23 times out of 34 matches, but he went down with an injury to the right quad. "I am going to keep fighting," said Nadal.

Upon victory, Roger Federer lifted his fifth Australian Open title and said, "I'm out of words, and Rafa said so many great things… I'd like to congratulate Rafa on an amazing comeback. I don't think either of us thought we'd be in the finals when we were at your academy four or five years ago. I'd just like to thank my team. It's been a different last six months. I didn't think I was going to make it here." Well, Australian Open 2017 was not only Federer's fifth but his first after the 2010 games.

Taking in Federer's victory, Nadal congratulated Federer and added, "It is amazing how he is playing after all this time away from the tour. For me, it has been a great month. It has been unforgettable." Nadal said further, "Today was a great match. Roger deserved it a bit more than me. I'm just going to keep trying. I feel I am back at a very high level, so I'm going to carry on fighting the whole season."

As usual, the first set started with Federer and Nadal sizing each other up. They played on familiar grounds and terms with neither ready to concede any early points to the other with their serves. They both focused on backhand winds to open up the court all through to the sixth set. They dragged on at 3-3 baseline till Nadal made some erroneous judgment. Nadal hit a serve straight into court while Federer rallied the serve with a forehand volley to achieve two breakpoints.

However, it didn't take quite 35 minutes before Federer set the pace as a clear leader. Federer quickly secured the first set with a 6-4 lead. Nadal was not ready to be caught pants down, he took on break-points, hoping to convert his serves but ended up with a 15/40 and 5-3 win in favor of Federer.

It, however, didn't just happen as a fluke for Federer. Each party worked hard to restrict the opponent's forehand even into the seventh game. But at some point in the competition, Federer launched an unexpected backhand and an unreturnable forehand to secure the first break, taking Nadal by storm.

Nadal intensified his play adopting untimely breaks to thwart Federer's strikes during the second set. Both parties continued their attacks, posing mid or early breaks to put the other party on the defensive. At some point, Nadal made some feverish serve that further helped increase the error margins against Federer. Nadal won six of the initial seven points. As Federer approached the net, Nadal made an intense groundstroke that unsettled Federer.

Nadal took his first serve that led to an inappropriate forehand and 2-0. Thus Nadal attained 30/0 but lost the three points and desperately tried to save Federer's two breaks to a 0-4. But Federer picked up points at 30/40 as Nadal went on the offensive, releasing a forehand that was countered by Federer with a swift forehand to an open court and then a break.

During the third set, Federer couldn't run a straight course in the match. Thus Nadal went on straight five points at 40/0 but eventually lost an attempt to convert three breakpoints with Federer striking an ace at each point to secure a 2-0 lead against Nadal.

Federer's backhand half volley running a line to 30/30 unsettled Nadal's deep backhand and ran for a forehand at the open court. He had a break once though placing Nadal under unparalleled pressure to a 3-0. A backhand and quick movement, followed by a forehand in succession, Nadal had too much to handle as he drove a volley winner to end the game at 6-3 within 42 minutes. Federer, for the first time, took Nadal on by leading two sets up against one.

With a mesmerizing forehand, Federer was able to make an early break during the fourth set and fourth game. Nadal rallied some points and took some clean serves, and a little lapse from Federer proved fatal to his early game. Struggling back up from 15/40, Federer made a go for the net to rally a low backhand and ended up overstretching and volleyed to the net. Nadal did a crosscourt to set a forehand winner.

At full stretch, Federer from a crosscourt angle did a backhand to secure a 4-1 point, Federer went for a 3-5 win. But in all, he made some erroneous judgments that made Federer appear invincible. On his part, Federer made good use of three break points and a sliced winner using his forehand to come home with a 4-1 win. Meanwhile, Nadal had already secured three wins from five sets.

Federer had taken on the game with so much zest while Nadal stood up to the challenge. The result was a knee injury that saw Federer requiring medical attention for a few minutes before the fifth set's commencement. Nadal stayed put, hopping about the court and waiting for the slightest opportunity. He eventually took it out on Federer's serve, rallying a signature forehand to secure an early break.

Federer didn't let it go. Instead, he rallied a break back to lock things up at 3-3 at the sixth game from Nadal's earlier 3-1 lead, although this wasn't until after Nadal had dealt some decisive blows and breakpoint to clinch a win. Federer rallied Nadal's backhand early enough to save one breakpoint. However, Federer made a forehand error that cost him a 30/40 break and three breakpoints by Nadal.

Nadal moved fast to even things out at 3-4 when he came from 0/40 to save four breakpoints. After leveling things up, Nadal was already exacerbated and began to lose composure. He made a faulty double that landed in the middle as Federer made him pull out to chase a forehand heading for the net. Federer then rallied two saves to reach two break points to concede a final break and win at last.

Within 30 minutes of receiving strikes and attacks from Nadal, Federer was 1-3 in defeat during the fifth set. But he somehow rose to stop the final charge from Nadal to emerge the winner. Both opponents had a better understanding of each person's play, heightening the play's tension. Federer, however, made two breakpoint serves to place Nadal further behind. Already Nadal had lost too much ground to Federer.

In a state of ecstasy, Federer leaped into the air to celebrate his 18th Grand Slam victory. Next, he turned around to console his long-time friend and rival, Nadal and broke down in tears. Federer says, "Tennis is a tough sport... there are no draws. If there were, I would have been happy to accept one and share it with Rafa."

Federer's wife, Mirka, and other teammates could not hold back the joy as it was a time for jubilation.

In the end, Federer had 73 wins comprised of 20 aces and 76 percent wins. Nadal had 4/17 breakpoint wins, a whopping 28 erroneous plays.

Federer admits, "I don't think either of us believed we'd be in the finals." Speaking to Nadal, Federer said, "I'm happy for you. I would have been happy to lose, to be honest. The comeback was as perfect as it was."

In response, Nadal says, "Today was a great match... so I'm going to carry on fighting the whole season."

For years, the duo had been at it with Nadal beating Federer on some other occasions over the years. As the clock begins to click for Federer, his winning streaks keep getting better, and the process more natural.

Australian Open 2017 presented the best of five sets with defending champion Novak Djokovic losing out. There were 128 competitors, 16 qualifiers and 8 wildcards in the five sets of the 105th edition.

SUMMARY:

- Final: Federer defeated Rafael Nadal- 6-4 3-6 6-1 3-6 6-3
- 126th Edition
- Games Won: 155
- Games Lost: 111
- Sets lost: 7
- Total time on the court: 17 hours 18 minutes
- Top 10 opponents defeated: Rafael Nadal (9), Kei Nishikori (5), Stan Wawrinka (4)
- Coach: Ivan Ljubicic and Severin Luthi

CHAPTER NINETEEN: GRAND SLAM 19

WIMBLEDON 2017

In 2013, about 14 years before Wimbledon 2017, Roger Federer won his first Grand Slam title against Mark Philippoussis. Then in 2017, he still had his winning streak going. Federer turned 36 a few days after Wimbledon 2017, but he still had his groove going.

"Wimbledon was always my favorite tournament. It will always be my favorite tournament. My heroes walked the grounds here and walked the courts here. Because of them, I think I became a better player too," says Federer.

Wimbledon 2017 was Federer's eighth title, and 19th Grand Slam win, but this time against Croatian tennis giant Marin Cilic at the finals. The game ended in 6-3, 6-1, 6-4 in a straight-set, which was not so much of a stiff contest for Federer. It was a less challenging competition for Federer than the Australian Open 2017 and Wimbledon 2012 against Nadal Rafael and Andy Murray respectively. Wimbledon 2017 opened the door for Federer to become the first player since Wimbledon 1976 to emerge the winner with a straight-set win like Bjorn Borg of 1976.

Between the 2013 and 2016 seasons, Federer suffered five heart-rending losses during the semi-final stage and only secured three tickets to the finals. He also had a knee injury he sustained while bathing his lovely twin girls. As a result, Federer underwent a torn meniscus surgery that kept him out of the game for about a month immediately after the Australian Open.

Federer took on Cilic with as much agility as he has always done. He also had a 6-1 lead, head-to-head to his credit, but needed to be cautious of Cilic's big-hitting ability. The game got so tense that Cilic was reported to have broken down in tears during the second set following a 3-0 loss while the second oldest men's winner at almost 36 years worked every angle in the court. Marin Cilic was the younger version of Federer at 28 years but couldn't take the heat from Federer, who was fast and furious!

Marin Cilic entered the game with all hopes high. He knew quite alright who he had to face, but the Croatian also had his winning antecedents to his credit. If for nothing, being the US Open 2014 champion and having defeated Federer during the quarterfinals could count for something. Well, Cilic broke down in tears before the end of the game and sobbed uncontrollably with his head buried in his towel as he witnessed the title slip away even before the end of the games.

At the kick-off after the second set, Cilic made a serve to rally Federer to the mid-courts, but Federer envisaged his move and did a counter to stretch the lead further by 4-1. Cilic, at some point at 6-1, requested a medical timeout and received painkillers and got his left foot bandaged.

However, Cilic pulled a stunt during the fourth game. He took advantage of a breakpoint during the fourth game, which should have placed Federer a point, but the Swiss sports giant rose to the challenge, dampening Cilic's chances.

At the fifth game, Federer countered Cilic's move with a break, which caused Cilic to weaken his offensive. Then, Federer made two unbeatable serves to claim an opener at 6-3 due to Cilic's error, which was his second in the finals.

It appears that Cilic lost his winning charm against Federer. At the close of the second set, Cilic had only two aces to his credit compared to other games where he would have fired over 130 shots in round six. It was swift, spontaneous, and full of intrigues, the fighting spirit, and a sheer will to survive. Finally, the 19th Grand Slam title went to Roger Federer after 1 hour 41 minutes of play.

Being the Greatest of All Time doesn't exonerate one from making considerable blunders. And these were some of the laughable scenarios that played out during the game against Cilic. For example, Federer double-faulted his first two serves during the games, just as he had to deal with an initial breakpoint at the fourth. Finally, though, Cilic netted a return that gave Federer a chance at 17 points in a row after he served.

For Cilic, it was another teary moment after investing so many preparations and hopes. "I gave it my best, that's all I could do," said Cilic.

Federer got his first major title in 2003 and followed through for the next three years. He won the title again in 2009 and 2012 but lost the title in 2014 and 2015 to Novak Djokovic.

However, Federer has all the accolades he could ever need to bring a rewarding career to an end, but not him. As his days in the game gradually wind to a halt, Federer says, "I love to play. (I have a) wonderful team. My wife's totally fine with me still playing. She's my number one supporter. She's amazing. I love playing big stages still. I don't mind the practice. I don't mind the travels. The goal is definitely to be here (Wimbledon) again next year to try and defend."

Just in case you have lost the will to go on in life, let the life and times of Roger Federer inspire you to dream again. He says, when talking with reporters from the Associated Press, "I always believed that I could maybe come back and do it again. And if you believe, you can go really, really far in your life, and I did that, and I'm happy I kept on believing and dreaming, and here I am today for the eighth. It's fantastic."

Writing Federer off too soon was a mistake some made too early. Yes, he had some rough moments healthwise, but he did the smart thing, and that was to take some time away from the game. When Federer returned to the court in January at Wimbledon 2017, it was like he never left in the first place.

The father of two sets of twins, twin girls aged 7, and twin boys aged 3, his kids love the games. And his love and passion, dexterity, and dominance of the game live on even into Australian Open 2018!

SUMMARY:

- Final: Federer defeated Marin Cilic - 6-3 6-1 6-4
- Edition: 131st Open Era
- Games Won: 122
- Games Lost: 74
- Sets lost: 0
- Total time on the court: 11 hours 37 minutes
- Top 10 opponents defeated: Marin Cilic (6), Milos Raonic (7)
- Coach: Ivan Ljubicic and Severin Luthi

CHAPTER TWENTY: GRAND SLAM 20

AUSTRALIAN OPEN 2018

The Australian Open 2018 finals presented another avenue for Cilic to redeem his image against Federer. At the same time, Federer came out to defend his title with the hopes of securing the 20th Grand Slam singles title. Cilic, on the other hand, had a chance to take on the Swiss sports giant to claim the victory and flush out the merciless defeat at Wimbledon 2017.

At 36 years, Federer took on 29-year-old Marin Cilic to secure another victory after five sets of fierce battles for the title. Federer finally clinched the title with 6-2, 6-7(5), 6-3, 3-6, 6-1 to equal sixth Australian Open titles for the men's singles. This victory places Federer at par with Novak Djokovic and Roy Emerson's sixth Australian Open. He made history by becoming the first male player with a win of six titles from two Grand Slam competitions, which includes six Australian Open titles and eight Wimbledon championships. That year's competition also placed Federer as the oldest male to secure a Grand Slam singles victory at the Open Era after Ken Rosewall's 1972 victory. Australian Open 2018 also marked the 10th Grand Slam title defense Federer faced since the 2008 US Open. It was the first, which marked the first time a Croatian player ever reached the Australian Open singles final.

Rafael Nadal had a go at the title against Federer for the No. 1 singles ranking but lost out at the quarter final stage due to a knee injury. He had slugged it out with Federer but only made it to the fourth round of the tournament.

Unlike the last competition, Federer had a smooth ride against Cilic during the first set that lasted only 24 minutes. He held sway with two out of three break points and got up to 92 percent with his first serve. His second serve was not so different as he secured 83 percent conversion, and 59 wins in the second serve to result in a tiebreak with Cilic.

However, the winning trend didn't continue for Federer in the second serve, but still, he somehow was able to record eight wins and seven aces. He also secured one breakpoint long enough to make the fourth set. The pressure to secure a win began to build on Federer as he lost some of his magical charms. Federer literally started making more errors than expected. This saw the greatest player of all time barely escaping with 36 percent of the first serve from the fourth set to win about 67 percent. Thus while Cilic had 13 wins to his credit, Federer was only able to hit a six-win.

In the third set, the ugly trend continued for Federer, following his abysmal performance from the second serve. And he says, "I wouldn't say I gave up hope, but I would have been happy with one major before I retired. I would have taken that. Now, I've got two more, maybe a third. One match away. We will see what happens."

However, during the fifth set, Cilic missed two chances to stop Federer from advancing when he couldn't break Federer's serve during the first game. Cilic blew those chances and then did a double-fault two times during the second game. By dropping his serves, he finally helped Federer ascend the tables against him.

In the first minutes of the game, Federer already aced the game with 15-0 while Cilic did a forehand wide with 30-0. At this point, Cilic was a bit perturbed and missed another forehand wide to give Federer another three life-changing points. As the pressure mounted, Federer missed his first serve in the fifth set. Then he rallied another serve straight unto Cilic's backhand that should have been a plus for Cilic, but he wasn't well-positioned to make the return at 0-40. Cilic put up a fight to edge the ball away. He tried working Federer to a 40-30 with a forehand. It ended up with a deuce when Federer returned a challenge or second long serve from Cilic. It was a breakpoint instead, and Federer's backhand converted it briskly. Cilic immediately with a forehand netted the ball as he dropped a serve! So, what were the outcomes? Game Over!

In ecstasy, Federer embraced Marin Cilic, acknowledging cheers from the now cheering crowd. Then he finally walked to a seat and began his customary weeping. Federer won his 20th Grand Slam title at age 35 and the sixth Australian Open title.

The game was tense in every way. Cilic wanted to secure his next title, but for Federer, it was more than just another title, it was another historical moment. Federer's fans at Rod Laver Arena didn't make the situation quite easy for Cilic either. They cheered Federer on to a 20th Grand Slam title win with every slight move he made. The crowd also seemed to celebrate Cilic's erroneous moves knowing fully well the implications for Federer.

The match went in an unprecedented manner. Both players had their clear chances but kept making errors at such critical points. Federer clearly could have won the game under three sets but somehow managed to allow the game to spill into five sets. Cilic had his chances, and he fought hard for a win. At the start of the fifth set, it looked like Cilic would win, but the tables suddenly turned. Still, he deserves commendation for his brilliant play and sportsmanship.

With a clear understanding of what it takes Federer said, "I know how hard it is to win on clay, how hard it is to win any major for that matter. It doesn't come around so easily. I was fighting so hard for so many years and ran into Novaks and Rafas and other great players along the way that blocked it for me for a while".

It doesn't take much to let the stream of tears flow from Federer's eyes. As the game ground to a halt and it was time to present the trophy to him, Federer's eyes became teary. "I'm so happy… winning is an absolute dream come true".

Meanwhile, Marin Cilic took over as the World No. 3 after Grigor Dimitrov. In a calm tone, he said, "Big congratulations to Roger and his team. It's amazing what you do year after year. All the best for

2018. Today was a tough match. I had a slight chance at the start of the fifth set. But Roger played an unbelievable fifth set." And so the cookie crumbles!

Federer's Grand Slam wins are no small feat. The Greatest Of All Time secures one French Open victory, five US Open, and eight wins at Wimbledon. By records, he is the 4th tennis player and the first man to secure 20 Grand Slam wins ever.

SUMMARY:

- Final: Federer defeated Marin Cilic - 6-2 6-7 (5) 6-3 3-6 6-1
- Edition: 106th
- Open Era Edition: 50th
- Games Won: 132
- Games Lost: 82
- Sets lost: 2
- Total time on the court: 13 hours 53 minutes
- Top 10 opponents defeated: Marin Cilic (6)
- Coach: Ivan Ljubicic and Severin Luthi

FINAL WORDS

This book is not a tribute to the Greatest of All Times in the tennis world, Roger Federer, but a compendium of his giant strides. It is about a man who knows how to pick his battles and decide which course to take.

Although a skilled player, he is not necessarily the best striker or has the best forehand, backhand, and serve. Nevertheless, Roger Federer is a die-hard and impeccable tennis player. Federer came, saw, and conquered. He has played in no less than 1,500 matches, producing 20 Grand Slam singles titles out of 31 finals and over 103 career wins. Federer has over 10 consecutive finals plus another 8 finals, which account for the two longest wins in the annals of tennis history.

Federer's sojourn in the game does not end there as he made it to 46 semi-final matches as well as 57 quarter-final appearances. He remains the tennis player with the highest record of all four Grand Slam wins in a year.

Official records show that Roger Federer of Switzerland has 20 Grand Slam titles, Rafael Nadal from Spain comes second place with 19 Grand Slam titles. Novak Djokovic of Serbia comes third with 17 Grand Slam titles. Pete Sampras of the United States of America comes fourth with 14 Grand Slam titles, while Roy Emerson of Australia holds 12 titles.

Both in and out of the field of play, Federer is an exciting and intriguing person. If nothing else, Federer's love and passion for the game transcend acquiring trophies. He plays well, works efficiently with his teammates, and holds nothing against his opponents. Just as he has enough tears to go round, Federer has a heart for other players. Every win for him is a privilege and not a right. He works hard to secure his victories and believes others have equal rights to the title. He is also one player with little to no controversy about his personal life or any dirt to smear his image.

Federer is undoubtedly a legend, a sports lover, a caring husband, and a caring father of two sets of twins. His entrance in the tennis world tells the story of one who did not allow the shortcomings of his life, injuries, and opponents to bring an end to his dream. Federer stood tall against all the odds to make his fans and family proud.

Printed in Great Britain
by Amazon

51681149R00064